ISBN 978-0-266-88413-2
PIBN 10904312

A Century and a Quarter of Service:
A History of the
Murfreesboro Baptist Church,
1848-1973

by

Raymond Hargus Taylor

aided
by

Antoinette White Hollomon
and
Ethleen Babb Underwood

Written on the Occasion of the 125th
Anniversary of the Church, and
Printed by the Chowan College
School of Graphic Arts

1973

dedicated to all those men and women
of the Murfreesboro Baptist Church —
past and present — for whom the
attempt to "keep covenant" with God
and one another has been a daily care

TABLE OF CONTENTS

Foreword

If a survey were taken to determine the more popular areas of study, it is improbable that the study of history would rank very high on the resulting scale. The judgment that "history is dry" accompanies many of us from the grammar school to the grave. Yet, we are all heirs of some particular history; some "past" which has shaped (if not determined) the "present" in which we live. We can neither understand and appreciate the "present," fully, nor anticipate the "future," wisely, without reference to that "past" which has gone before.

A Century And A Quarter Of Service: A History Of The Murfreesboro Baptist Church, 1848-1973 has been written in an effort to illuminate that churchly heritage associated with the life and work of this particular congregation. The primary resource materials used in the preparation of this writing have been the *Minutes* of Church Conference.[1] Such records have been supplemented by reference to the official records of the church and her work,[2] and personal conversation with various current members of the church and congregation.[3]

---

[1]The *Minutes* vary greatly in the fulness and detail with which they record the business of the church throughout the years of her life and work. As a general rule: the earlier the records, the greater the fidelity to detail on the part of church clerks. There are exceptions to the rule, however, both early and late.

[2]Of particular note here are the following manuscript accounts: (1) "History of the Murfreesboro Baptist Church," compiled in 1930 by Herman H. Babb, Mrs. George T. Underwood, and Mrs. E. B. Vaughan; (2) "History of Murfreesboro Baptist W. M. S.," written by Mrs. P. D. Sewell in 1939 upon the occasion of the 50th anniversary of the Society; and (3) "History of the Baptist Church, Also of the Beginning of W. M. U," also prepared by Mrs. Sewell.

[3]In this regard the writer is especially grateful for information and data

In the compilation of this particular account of the life and work of the Murfreesboro Baptist Church, special credit and appreciation are due Mrs. G. Roger Hollomon and Mrs. R. Harry Underwood — members, along with the writer, of the History Committee — for their contributions to this volume. Mrs. Hollomon did extensive research, especially with regard to the work of Woman's Missionary Union. She has also been extremely helpful to a relatively "late comer" to the Murfreesboro Baptist Church in furnishing data regarding particular individuals whom she has known over a long tenure as a member of the church and community.

Mrs. Underwood has been of invaluable aid in procuring certain written records—including materials prepared by Mrs. P. D. Sewell, and including a copy of the history of the church written by Herman H. Babb, Mrs. George T. Underwood, and Mrs. E. B. Vaughan. She has also been of significant aid in the final preparation of the rosters of church members, and in the reading of proofs before handing the materials over in final form to the printers.

While the aid of these persons — and many others — is freely acknowledged, all responsibility for any errors and/or omissions must be charged to the writer. He has attempted to include that which seemed of most significance, given the time at his disposal for the praparation of this account and the quality of the records available.

A Century And A Quarter Of Service: A History Of The Murfreesboro Baptist Church, 1848-1973 is presented to the reader in the hope that he may derive but a small measure of that pleasure and profit from pursuing it which the writer and his associates have derived from its preparation.

October 1973   Raymond Hargus Taylor

---

derived through conversations with Mrs. G. R. Hollomon, Mrs. R. Harry Underwood, Mrs. Thomas B. Wynn, and Mrs. W. E. Deanes, Sr.

Chapter 1

The Beginnings, 1842-1848

The Church worshiping at Parker's Meeting House (Meherrin Church) remained the only constituted organization of the Baptist denomination within the bounds of the present Hertford County from the early 1730s until the opening decade of the nineteenth century.[1] "Branches" of this church — gathered for occasional worship in the vicinities of Ahoskie, Maney's Neck, and Winton — had grown sufficiently strong to be constituted as independent bodies by 1804, 1835, and 1839, respectively.[2] But the town of Murfreesboro, which had been incorporated in 1787, was to continue without a Baptist meeting house for almost a half-century after her incorporation through legislative act of the General Assembly.[3]

There were families of Baptist persuasion and inclination living

[1]The designation "the Church worshiping at Parker's Meeting House" continued in popular usage for some years after the "reformation" in the church (c. 1793) and her subsequent admission into the Kehukee Baptist Association. In strict Baptist usage, the Church (the people) is always distinguished from the "place" to which the people repair for worship (the meeting house in a particular place).

[2]These three churches are First Baptist Church, Ahoskie; Buckhorn Baptist Church; and Mt. Tabor Baptist Church.

[3]Meherrin has remained, essentially, a "rural" church throughout her history. It is only in recent years, of course, that the Murfreesboro town limits have been extended to the site of the Meherrin Church building.

in the town, to be sure. But the proximity of Parker's Meeting House — combined with a strong sense of loyalty to this Mother Church of the Baptists in the region — served to forestall earlier attempts which might have been made at establishing a "town" church independent of Meherrin. Two events, however, were destined to precipitate the call for "setting off" a branch of the Meherrin Church, gathered in Murfreesboro. The first was the moving of the Reverend George M. Thompson,[4] with his family, to a house within the town limits. The second — and more significant — event was the outbreak of revival in Murfreesboro and vicinity in June 1842.

Thompson began to hold occasional evening services in the town after 1840. This, undoubtedly, heightened the interest in having a Baptist house of worship in the town. But the effects of revival were determinative. A contemporary account of the revival season reads as follows:

On Sunday (5th of June 1842,) our pastor preached to a large audience at our meeting house in the suburbs, and we trust not without effect. At candle-lighting Elder Robert McNabb preached by invitation for us, in the Presbyterian church. Up to this time, christians had been very lukewarm, although ministers of different denominations had labored faithfully for our benefit. Among our own ministry were Bishop Hume, and the reverend President of Wake Forest College, had been with us on two occasions, and other ministers of note, among the Methodists and Presbyterians had labored in the place. Prospects in the commencement of the meeting were gloomy. On Monday (the next day) a prayer-meeting was

---

[4]George Matthias Thompson (1803-1850) was a native of London, England. His family emigrated to New York City in 1815. Coming south in 1828, Thompson was ordained to the ministry in Richmond, Virginia, and soon thereafter settled in Pasquotank County. There he served the churches at Salem, Elizabeth City, and Suffolk, Virginia, before assuming the pastoral charge of the Meherrin Church in 1838. He died on November 27, 1850, in Halifax County, en route to the meeting of the Baptist State Convention of North Carolina in Louisburg. His remains were buried in the garden of his home in Murfreesboro.

appointed to be held at 4 p.m., at which only six persons were present, and four of them were non-professors. The meetings were kept up until the 11th, when one person was enabled to make a profession. Meetings now became more interesting, people came out, and services were held at sunrise, at 8 A. M., 11 A. M., 4 P. M., and at 8 P. M.; indeed the house of God was scarcely without worshippers, at any hour of the day. Religion became a matter of universal concern; merchants closed their doors, mechanics quit their shops; and notwithstanding the rain descended in torrents during the meeting, the church was thronged, and many in the throng were the most feeble and delicate ladies in the village.[5]

In the wake of this revival season, and upon petition of certain members residing in the town of Murfreesboro, Meherrin Church was authorized the "setting off" of a "branch church . . . to be governed by their own laws, provided they are not inconsistent with our laws and articles,"[6] and with the understanding that the branch church would report its actions quarterly to the parent body[7] On July 18, 1842, this fledgling body held its first conference in the home of N. H. Hodges,[8] with G. M. Thompson

---

[5]This account — prepared for the *Southern Christian Repository* — is repeated in Samuel J. Wheeler's *History of the Baptist Church Worshipping at Parker's Meeting House, Called Meherrin* (Raleigh: Recorder Office, 1847), pp. 41-42. Robert McNabb, an evangelist of some note, resided in Granville County in 1842. Bishop Hume (Thomas Hume, Sr.) was pastor of Court Street Baptist Church, Portsmouth, Virginia. The "reverend President" of Wake Forest would have been Samuel Wait.

[6]*Minutes* of Meherrin Baptist Church Conference, July 2, 1842. The account used here was copied by Thomas A. Brett, and is found on page 158 of Church Record Book I of the Murfreesboro Baptist Church.

[7]On occasion the Meherrin Church had to remind the Murfreesboro branch of her obligations in this regard.

[8]Hodges, a convert in the revival of June-July 1842, had been baptized on July 7, 1842, by McNabb. He was not to remain in the good graces of the church for very long, however, being expelled in September 1843 for "unchristianlike conduct and undue levity . . . ."

acting as moderator. For purposes of proceeding with the proper
"ordering" of the church, Lewis T. Spiers[9] was elected clerk;
James H. Lassiter,[10] treasurer. A committee consisting of Samuel
J. Wheeler,[11] Samuel Polkinhorn,[12] and Spiers was authorized
to draw up "Rules of Decorum."[13] It was agreed that church
conference would be held on Thursday evening before the 1st
Lord's day in each month.[14]

Succeeding monthly conferences through November 1842 were
conducted in the Male Academy building, while attempts were
being made to secure the aid of the Mt. Tabor and Buckhorn
churches in soliciting subscriptions towards the erection of a per-

---

[9]Lewis T. Spiers, another convert of the 1842 revival, was to become a
prominent leader in the Murfreesboro Baptist Church, serving for several
years as clerk and as superintendent of the Sunday School.

[10]James H. Lassiter was to become one of the first deacons elected by
the Murfreesboro Church in 1848. He moved to Henderson, North Carolina,
during or shortly after the Civil War, where he became a respected leader
in First Baptist Church, Henderson. His name last appears in the Murfreesboro records in 1862.

[11]Samuel Jordan Wheeler (1810-1879) lived in the town and often
worshiped with the Murfreesboro congregation, but he chose to remain
with Meherrin when the town church was constituted in 1848. A medical
doctor, Wheeler served as clerk of the Meherrin Baptist Church and of
the Chowan Baptist Association for many years. He was a talented and
prolific writer, both for the denominational and the secular presses.

[12]Samuel Polkinhorn (or Polkinhome) had been baptized by McNabb
in July 1842. Though elected a deacon in 1848, there is no record of his
ordination or future service in this capacity. His name disappears from the
church records after the constitution of the Murfreesboro Church in 1848.

[13]See Apendix A. The Rules of Decorum were used as a guide to the
orderly conduct of church conference

[14]*Minutes of Murfreesboro Baptist Church Conference*, July 18, 1842.
Hereafter cited as *Minutes*, with the appropriate date indicated. These
Minutes are found in two large volumes of Murfreesboro Baptist Church
Record Books, housed for safekeeping in the Whitaker Library of Chowan
College. They cover the period, 1842-1950. The earlier portion of these
records was copied by T. A. Brett, Church Clerk in 1886, from a previous
record book which is now lost. It was probably the book kept by Lewis
T. Spiers, the first Church Clerk.

manent meeting house.[15] At a called conference on December 6, 1842, a committee reported favorably on the attempt to purchase a lot from John W. Southall. Thompson, Wheeler, Lassiter, and Jacob W. Parker[16] were appointed trustees to obtain a deed for the property and were empowered to "instruct the building Committee to go forward with the building of the Church as fast as they have means in hand belonging to the Church."[17]

Construction of the new meeting house began in May 1843. Meanwhile, a finance committee continued to solicit and collect subscriptions to underwrite the full cost of the construction. The building was sufficiently completed by November to warrant a service of dedication. Accordingly, the Reverend E. L. Magoon[18] of Richmond, Virginia, preached the dedicatory sermon on November 5, 1843. The winter season and the remaining work to be done on the interior of the building, however, prevented the holding of conference and — presumably — services of worship in the new house of worship until April 1844. A stove was not purchased until the autumn following.[19]

Samuel J. Wheeler, again, provides a contemporary account of the circumstances, along with a graphic description of the first meeting house built by the Baptist Church in Murfreesboro:

> The undertaking [i.e., the building of a meeting house] was commenced under circumstances extremely inauspicious. Besides the weakness of the body in a pecuniary point of view, the church was still burdened with a portion of the debt incurred by the erection of a meeting house of the mother church in 1842. The project was

---

[15]*Minutes,* November 1842.

[16]Jacob W. Parker was to become the first treasurer of the Murfreesboro Baptist Church in 1848. His name appears last in the records of church conference in July 1852. The earliest "church roll" has the notation after his name: "out without record."

[17]*Minutes,* December 6, 1842.

[18]Elias Lyman Magoon was pastor of Second Baptist Church, Richmond, 1839-1845. He left his Richmond pastorate in consequence of his sentiments opposing a division of the denomination over the slavery issue.

[19]*Minutes,* October 31, 1844.

denounced by some as absurd. It was however undertaken, relying upon a good providence. Commissioners were, Rev. G. M. Thonipson, brethren S. J. Wheeler, S. Polkinhorn, and Messers. L. M. Cowper and Perry Carter. Bryan Bishop, an architect of some taste, was appointed to superintend the erection of the house . . . The house is admired by good judges, for its thorough consistency with the principles of correct architecture. Its exterior is constructed after the model of the Erectheum at Athens: the front exhibiting an entablature embellished with a rich cornice, 13 inches in depth, supported on four columns of the Tuscan order. On entering the church a vestibule is traversed, extending the whole breadth of the church, 8 feet deep. A well-constructed frieze and architrave surround the building on three sides; the stylobate consisting of a broad flight of steps, descends in front on either hand to the plinth, a solid piece firmly embedded. The Vestibule supports the belfry, ten feet in height and eight feet square: its upper part surrounded by a balustrade, the four columns of which support, each one, an urn. A spire arises from the belfry, with the usual appendage of a ball and a dart. Dimensions of the building are 32 by 48 feet; height from the foundation to the end of the spire 81 feet; size of the ball 22 inches in diameter; length of the dart 6 feet. The roof is a self supporting roof, so that no columns are seen from within to diminish the view of the upper part of the interior. The house is well ventilated by ten windows containing 48 panes of glass each; provided with a bell, stove and other appurtenances necessary for the comfort of a worshipping people. It is proposed by some members to apply to the mother church for permission to be erected into an independent church.[20]

Agitation for constituting the Murfreesboro congregation into an independent church likely began with the completion of a

---

[20]Wheeler, *op. cit.*, pp. 29-31.

meeting house in the town. The first reference to such, however, is not recorded until November 1846, when a committee was appointed to "make a report on the propriety of constituting this Branch into an independent Church." The matter was postponed "indefinitely" one month later.[21] Meanwhile, the infant congregation continued to minister to the Baptists living in Murfreesboro: conducting worship,[22] receiving and disciplining members,[23] engaging in prayer meetings and the work of a Sabbath School,[24] and seeking to strengthen its financial resources.[25]

But the plea for constituting a church in Murfreesboro — independent of the congregation worshiping at Meherrin — was not to go unheeded for very long. In mid-1848 another committee was appointed to "inquire into the expediency" of constituting an independent church. Two weeks later this committee reported favorably. Whereupon William E. Poole,[26] Jacob Parker, and Lewis Spiers

---

[21]*Minutes,* November 1846; December 1846. This committee was composed of Wheeler, Lassiter, and Lassiter, and Lewis Spiers. Wheeler made the motion to "postpone indefinitely."

[22]There is no indication of the frequency with which services of worship were scheduled and conducted. Since the pastoral services of Thompson, were shared with Meherrin, Mt. Carmel, and (for a time) Potecasi, it must be assumed that services in the town were occasional or infrequent. In 1847 Meherrin reported services on the 1st and 3rd Lord's days in each month; Mt. Carmel, on the 4th Lord's day; and Potecasi, on the 2nd Lord's day!

[23]Records indicate that the church received 7 members, dismissed 1 (by letter), and excluded 2 between August 1842 and November 1848.

[24]Prayer meetings are not mentioned in the records before August 1848, though the reference seems to be to a change in time and/or frequency of such meetings. Men and women were urged to attend the Sabbath School in June 1847, with Thompson requested to make "suitable remarks thereon" from the pulpit. Samuel J. Wheeler had begun a Sabbath School at Meherrin as early as 1833. He suggests that a School was meeting in Murfreesboro by 1843.

[25]The church had no treasury, as such. Monies were received to meet specific needs as these arose. The common practice was to name a committee to solicit gifts or subscriptions towards defraying the cost of a particular project, with a "treasurer" appointed to receive the funds as they were raised.

[26]Stepson of George M. Thompson.

were appointed to write a petition "to be presented to all the white members living in town for their signature." The constitution was appointed for the 3rd Lord's day in November, with Elders James McDaniel, W. H. Jordan, Thomas Meredith, J. J. Finch, Q. H. Trotman, James Delke, C. R. Hendrickson, and A. M. Craig to be invited to attend and to participate in the services of the day.[27]

The Church at Meherrin concurred with the request of the petitioners at her monthly conference in November 1848. Thus, the stage was set for the constitution of the Murfreesboro Baptist Church, with the solemn occasion appointed for November 19-20, 1848.[28]

The council of ministers and deacons assembled on November 19 for the purpose of "considering the propriety of constituting them [i.e., the Murfreesboro petitioners] into a Branch of Christ's Church" consisted of C. R. Hendrickson, William D. Pritchard,[29] Archibald McDowell,[30] G. M. Thompson, Samuel J. Wheeler, and A. J. Battle.[31] After appointing Henderickson moderator and Battle clerk, the assembly was led in prayer by McDowell. The names of those desiring to be constituted were read by Thompson, along with their Covenant

---

[27]Of these ministers to be invited, Quinton H. Trotman, James Delke, and Andrew M. Craig were serving churches in the Chowan Association. Charles R. Hendrickson had just assumed his pastoral duties with the church in Elizabeth City. Thomas Meredith, who had formerly served in the Chowan Association, was editor of the *Biblical Recorder*. Josiah J. Finch was pastor of the Baptist Church in Raleigh. James McDaniel — one of the "founders" of the Baptist State Convention — was pastor of the Baptist Church in Wilmington. William Hill Jordan — who had some claim to being a "local" man, since he had spent a portion of his youth in Murfreesboro — was residing in Warren County at this time.

[28]The names of thirty-one persons desiring to be constituted into a new church were read. Twenty-nine of these had petitioned for dismission from Meherrin. The names of Susan Banks and Angeline Spiers do not occur in the Meherrin record.

[29]Pritchard was clerk of First Baptist Church, Elizabeth City.

[30]McDowell had just come to Murfreesboro as principal of the newly established Chowan Baptist Female Institute. Though referred to as "Reverend" in this account, McDowell was not ordained until 1850.

[31]Amos Johnston Battle (1805-1870) was pastor of the Buckhorn Church and "Steward" of the Chowan Baptist Female Institute.

and Articles of Faith.[32] "On motion the brethren and sisters were declared to be qualified for being Constituted into an independent Branch of the Church of our Lord Jesus Christ."[33]

The order of service for the constituting of the church was set for Sunday, November 20, as follows: Hendrickson, to deliver the sermon; Battle, to offer the prayer; McDowell, to give a charge to the church; and Thompson to extend the right hand of fellowship to the members being constituted into the new church. With the council being satisfied as to the character and qualifications of the duly elected deacons — Benjamin A. Spiers and James H. Lassiter — a service of ordination of the same was scheduled for Sunday afternoon. On that occasion it was to be Battle who would preach the sermon; Thompson, offer the ordaining prayer; and Hendrickson, deliver a charge to both the deacons and the church.[34]

November 20, however, turned out to be such an unpleasant day that the services were postponed until Monday, November 21. They then proceeded as planned. The account of the event concludes with these words:

> At night the Rev. C. R. Hendrickson preached on the Communion of the Lord's Supper and with the assistance of the Rev. A. J. Battle, administered the Bread and Wine to this new Church and many visiting Brethren and

---

[32]See Appendix A.

[33]Pages 208-209 of Church Record Book I contain Thomas A. Brett's transcription of the constitutional meetings, taken from the "Old Record Book." The roster of visiting ministers present for the occasion does not correspond, fully, with the names of those who were to be invited. Some, obviously, were unable to attend. But an interesting item is found in the *Minutes*, October 1848, when the "Church approved the course of the Clerk in refusing to write certain Bishops to come to our aid in Constituting the Church in Murfreesboro." There is no indication of either those invitations witheld, or the reasons for witholding them.

[34]These men, along with Samuel Polkinhorn, had been elected deacons earlier in November. Benjamin Alexander Spiers (1818-1873) was the first Superintendent of the Sunday School following the constitution of the Murfreesboro Church. He was a frequent "delegate" of the church to the annual meetings of the Chowan Baptist Association.

Sisters, all of whom appeared to be deeply affected on this solemn occasion.

May God's blessing rest on all these interesting and soul affecting exercises.[35]

---

[35]Presumably the account of Lewis T. Spiers, as transcribed by Thomas A. Brett.

Chapter 2

The First Quarter-Century, 1848-1873:

The Pastorates of
Forey, Land, and McDowell

The first business of a newly constituted church is the calling of a pastor to minister with and among them. But the Murfreesboro Baptist Church was to take account of two other considerations before settling upon one to "go in and out" and minister among them. The first was to "ascertain what amount can be raised for the support of a pastor."[1] The second was to determine the frequency with which the church would seek to gather for services of worship. A committee—including the newly elected treasurer, Jacob Parker—was appointed to attend to the first matter during conference on November 29, 1848. At that same time, the body expressed consensus in desiring "the services of a Pastor on every Lord's day . . ."[2] When the committee to ascertain the amount of funds available for pastoral support made its report one month later, the church concluded, reluctantly, that while it might be expedient to have the services of a pastor on every Sunday, "for the want of funds, it was impracticable."[3]

At conference on January 23, 1849, the church issued a call

---

[1] *Minutes*, November 29, 1848.
[2] *Ibid.*
[3] *Ibid.*, December 19, 1848.

11

to the Reverend George M. Thompson. As was the custom, a committee was appointed to "wait upon Brother Thompson and inform him of the Call." This same committee, composed of James H. Lassiter and Lewis T. Spiers, was authorized to "wait on our brethren and Citizens to see what amount can be raised for his salary."[4] When the committee made its report at a succeeding conference, it was noted that their assignment had been carried out with reference to Thompson. Unfortunately, they had to report that he would "neither accept nor refuse the Call."[5]

Still entertaining the hope of securing the services of a pastor on every Lord's day, the church authorized Lassiter and Parker to attempt to ascertain—again—whether an amount sufficient to support a pastor for preaching every Sunday in the month could be subscribed. If—in their judgement—such was the case, they were further authorized to initiate a correspondence with Elder James D. Breed "with reference to his settlement with this Church."[6] The report of this committee on finances was later received, but the records give no indication of the substance of that report.[7]

By May 1, however, the prospects of gaining a pastor who could conduct services on every Lord's day had brightened considerably. The plan was to call as pastor of the church the man who would assume his duties in the days ahead as principal of the Chowan Female Institute. Accordingly, a call was extended to the Reverend M. R. Forey,[8] with a committee named to wait upon Forey and to notify

---

[4]*Ibid.*, January 23, 1849. Of fifteen votes cast, Thompson received 8; William P. Britton, 6. One ballot was unmarked.

[5]*Ibid.*, March 15, 1849. The delay of seven weeks probably indicates that Thompson may have been extremely reluctant to answer "No" to the committee, although he could hardly afford to relinquish other pastoral responsibilities in order to assume work in Murfreesboro.

[6]There is no indication that such correspondence was initiated.

[7]*Minutes*, May 1, 1849.

[8]Martin Rudolph Forey (1817-1881) was a native of the State of New York. He had attended Madison University (now Colgate) for two years before moving to South Carolina, where he became principal of Barnwell Academy. He was ordained to the ministry in 1848, becoming pastor of the Baptist Church in New Bern, North Carolina. He served for five years,

him of his election as pastor of the church. Forey was present in conference one month later, thus beginning his services as the first pastor of the Murfreesboro Baptist Church.[9]

M. R. Forey was to continue his pastoral responsibilities with the church for slightly more than two years. During his tenure, the church joined with her sister Baptist churches of the region in the life and work of the Chowan Baptist Association — an affiliation which was maintained until the Murfreesboro Church joined in forming the West Chowan Baptist Association in 1883. It must have been with considerable pride that she could note in her letter to the Chowan Association in 1851: services on every Sabbath — a claim which could only be made by three of the forty-seven churches in the association. She could also lay claim to a Sunday School consisting of ninety-three scholars and nine teachers in 1851. This record was then exceeded only by the schools sponsored by the church in Elizabeth City.[10]

Order and discipline were maintained, with a minimum of problems resulting from "disorderly walk" on the part of the mem-

---

1849-1854, as principal of Chowan Female Collegiate Institute. In 1854 he moved to Hampton, Virginia, where he founded Chesapeake Female College. By 1857 he had returned to New York, subsequently serving in churches in central New York, acting as General Agent for the ill-fated Chicago University, and later founded Judson University, in Judsonia, Arkansas.

[9]Just how early Forey became associated with the Institute is unclear. In mid-April, 1849, an occurence of small pox in Murfreesboro had prompted Archibald McDowell to suspend the operations of the school and, subsequently, to leave the town for a more healthful climate. By May 1, Forey was acting as principal pro tem, by authorization of the Executive Committee of the Board of Trustees. He represented the Murfreesboro Church as its pastor — though not yet a member of the church — at the meeting of the Chowan Association, May 17-20, 1849.

[10]The church applied for membership in the Chowan Association in May 1849. In the same year she affiliated with the Bertie Union — an association of Baptist churches in Bertie, Hertford, and Northampton counties which met quarterly for fellowship, and for discussion of mutual concerns. For certain annual statistical data reported to the Chowan and West Chowan associations, see Appendix D.

bers of the church.[11] Furnishings were added to the church building, with attention called to the work of the women of the church and town in this regard.[12] Several were added to the membership roll, with most of these being students of the Institute.[13] Death had claimed only two members during the first 2½ years of the church's life.[14] An early sign of that spirit of co-operation which was to maintain between Murfreesboro Baptist Church and the Chowan Baptist Female Institute was noted in mid-1851: "The use of the Church edifice was granted to the Principal for the celebration of the approaching anniversary of the C. B. F. Institute."[15]

One month later, however, Forey tendered his resignation as pastor, explaining that the "severe duties of his office" in the Institute made it impossible for him to maintain the dual roles of pastor and principal.[16] It was to be a year before a new pastor accepted the call of the Murfreesboro congregation. Meanwhile, the business of the church did not go unattended. Evidence of the vitality of the

---

[11]One member was excommunicated in 1851 due to "reports calculated to bring reproach on the Church." On the other hand, one member asked and received forgiveness when he expressed repentance for "engaging in a shooting match"; another, for some difficulty between him and a citizen of the town. The seriousness with which the church took its worship life is indicated by an item recorded in May 1851: "On Lord's day May 11th 1851 at 4 O'Clock P. M. Church met to celebrate the Lord's Supper: it is a matter of profound regret that several . . . of the brethren were absent, from the solemn service; notwithstanding their plighted Covenant vows; not to absent themselves from the Communion of the Lord's Supper."

[12]Repairs included work on the windows in the gallery, the addition of a door to the building, and painting the building. A committee of women was called upon to solicit funds to be used for carpeting the building.

[13]Of the 14 persons added to the church, May 1849-May 1851, at least 8 can be identified as students of the Institute.

[14]Unfortunately, there is no record of the names of these deceased members.

[15]*Minutes*, July 31, 1851.

[16]*Ibid.*, August 14, 1851. It is unclear whether Forey continued to preach for the congregation until his successor was named. His presence is noted at the church conferences during this interim, and he probably baptized the several new converts at the conclusion of the spring revival meeting in 1852.

congregation — even apart from pastoral leadership — is found in the fact that the first revival or protracted meeting was conducted in April-May, 1852, during which some "57 persons in the judgement of Charity passed from death unto life. . . ."[17]

A successor to Forey was found in the Reverend Robert H. Land, who was elected to the pastoral office in June 1852, and who began his services on the 4th Sunday in October.[18] He was to serve the church and congregation for approximately three years, during which time he was also Professor of Latin Language and Literature at Chowan. Land's coming necessitated a reduction in the frequency with which worship services would be conducted, however, the church reporting services on 2nd and 4th Sundays, only, in 1853.[19]

During Land's pastorate the church increased in membership to a high of 60 in 1853, but had declined to 50 by 1855. Major attention was given to continuing repairs and improvements to the church building and to the liquidation of debts incurred for incidental expenses.[20] The Sunday School — under the superintendency of B. A. Spiers — continued its functions, but had declined to an enrolment of only 46 "scholars" by 1855. The church's letter to

---

[17]This series of meetings extended from April 18 - May 12, with the Reverend John S. Reynoldson conducting the services. Reynoldson, who had been pastor of the Market Street Church, Petersburg, Virginia, was then devoting his full time to the work of an itinerant evangelist.

[18]Robert H. Land (1821-1881) was born in Sussex County, Virginia. He attended Richmond College and graduated from Columbian College (1847). He returned to Newville, Sussex County, from which place he moved to Murfreesboro. The remaining days of his ministry after leaving Murfreesboro were spent in King and Queen County, Virginia, where he served as pastor and also operated a boarding school known as Landon Seminary. A biographer speaks of both Land and his wife as being "exceedingly cultured and refined, with the polished manners of old-time Virginians."

[19]Land appears to have continued to serve a church in Sussex County throughout his stay in Murfreesboro. He was also pastor of the Jerusalem Church (Courtland) during a portion of his tenure with the Institute and the Murfreesboro congregation.

[20]*Minutes*, May 6, 1853; June 6, 1853; April 1, 1854. The steeple of the building had to undergo major repairs to eliminate leaking.

the association in 1855 did note, however, that services had been resumed on every Sunday in the month.

One of the most interesting — and unfortunate — cases of disciplinary action throughout the history of the church spanned the last year of Land's ministry. M. R. Forey had resigned his position with the Institute and had moved to Hampton, Virginia, prior to the conclusion of the spring term in 1854. When he applied to the church for a letter of dismission, a committee was appointed to "communicate . . . the reasons that constrain this Church to with-hold a letter of dismission from him."[21] The case continued until late 1856, when the charges against Forey were finally heard by a council of ministers meeting in Portsmouth, Virginia, on December 17, 1856. Upon the recommendation of this council, the Murfreesboro Church agreed to grant Forey's original request.[22]

In October 1855 the church elected to call a pastor who would prove to be the man destined to minister among them longer than any other person who held the pastoral office throughout the church's history.[23] This was the Reverend Archibald McDowell, who had just returned to the Chowan Baptist Female Institute at the invitation of William Hooper — Forey's successor in the presidency — as Professor of Mathematics and Natural Science. Born in Kershaw

---

[21] *Ibid.*, June 4, 1854.

[22] The church records do not indicate the nature of the church's grievances against Forey. Since Godwin Cotton Moore, Chairman of the Board of Trustees of the Institute, was called as a witness at Forey's hearing before the Portsmouth council, it can be inferred that Forey had made some comments regarding the managment of the Institute. On the other hand, Forey later produced a letter from T. B. Jones — moderator of the Portsmouth Council — indicating that the council had felt him guilty of keeping loose accounts and, perhaps, of indulging in certain imprudences due to the embarrassing financial situation of the Institute. At the same time, he was cleared of any intentional wrongdoing. Forey also charged the church of failing to keep its pledge with regard to his salary. A final settlement of the difficulties between Forey, the Institute, and the church had not been reached as late as 1870. See *Biblical Recorder*, August 3, 1870.

[23] Earlier historians have assumed that McDowell served continuously as pastor from the time of his initial call until 1880. This fails to take account of John Mitchell's "first" pastorate, 1873-1875.

District, South Carolina, on April 10, 1818, McDowell had entered Wake Forest College in 1842, and had graduated from that institution in 1847. He had become a deacon in the Wake Forest Church, had been licensed to preach while at Wake Forest, and is said to have entertained hopes of becoming a Christian missionary to foreign lands. It was also at Wake Forest that he wooed and won the hand of Mary Hayes Owen in marriage. Together they had come to Murfreesboro in October 1848 to open the Chowan Institute.

Of the two men (Hooper and McDowell), the former was undoubtedly the more gifted as a thinker, writer, and speaker. But McDowell possessed the energy, industry, and personality to be a good pastor. Thus, it was quite natural that the Murfreesboro congregation would turn towards him when seeking a successor to Land — continuing the practice of engaging an employee of the Institute to also serve as pastor of the church and congregation.

McDowell entered upon his labors with characteristic vigor. The church engaged in worship every Sunday, with McDowell's pastoral services spent on them alone. During each year of his pastorate — save four — he headed the delegation which represented the church in the annual meetings of the Chowan Association.[24] He and William Hooper were appointed delegates of the church to the 1856 session of the Baptist State Convention, the first recorded instance of the church's naming a delegation to this body.[25] Apart from his pastoral responsibilities, McDowell was kept busy with classroom and administrative duties, with maintaining meterological data for the Smithsonian Institute, occasional lecturing and preaching elsewhere, and with rather frequent correspondence for the *Biblical Recorder* and other religious periodicals.[26]

---

[24]McDowell was not present at the annual meetings in 1856, 1857, 1862, and 1872. Like many of the churches, Murfreesboro was not represented at the 1862 meeting.

[25]McDowell was Corresponding Secretary of the Convention in 1853, Recording Secretary in 1854, and preached the Introductory Sermon in both 1854 and 1865. He is also listed as a Life Member of the Convention, and held various other positions of trust and responsibility.

[26]The February 5, 1857, issue of the *Biblical Recorder* contains a letter from McDowell, giving a "short abstract" of his meterological observations

Church membership reached a high of 85 in 1862, before declining in the wake of the Civil War and its aftermath.[27] Most of the members remained faithful to their covenant vows, though the war years saw an increase in disciplinary action against those who severely tested their faith and the convenant.[28] Generally, the financial situation of the church appeared to be in better shape than in earlier years. Home Missions, Foreign Missions, and Education — the three primary "benevolent objects" of the Chowan Association and of the Baptist State Convention — could expect significant support from the Murfreesboro congregation.[29] Locally, the continuing need for repairs to the church edifice absorbed the largest expenditures.[30]

It was during McDowell's pastorate that Joseph E. Carter became the first "native son" of the church to enter the Gospel ministry. The only son of Perry and Priscilla Carter, Joseph Carter had united with the Murfreesboro Church in 1851. In 1858 he appeared before conference with the request that his name be erased from the church roll, "not regarding himself as worthy of member-

---

for the month of January. He records a snowfall of 10 inches and the "iceing over" of the Meherrin River to a thickness of 5 inches!

[27]Reports to the Chowan Association indicate that 98 persons were baptized into the membership of the church, 1856-1872. An additional 34 were received by letter. On the other hand, a total of 82 persons were reported as lost through dismissal, exclusion, or death during the same period.

[28]While only 2 persons had been excluded from the membership during the first ten years, 7 were excluded between 1859 and 1865.

[29]Associational records did not generally indicate gifts to benevolent objects prior to 1856. Gifts to Home Missions are reported for Murfreesboro in 1856 and 1857; to Foreign Missions, in 1856. In 1867 the church reported total pledges and/or gifts in the amount of $1,067, with $650 of that amount pledged to the endowment of Wake Forest College. In 1861 the Murfreesboro delegates to the Chowan Association had been instructed to "pledge this Church to an amount double that contributed by any other Church in behalf of the Chowan F[emale] Collegiate Institute."

[30]Attention had been called to needed repairs at conferences on June 4, 1856; March 13, 1858; and June 12, 1858. J. H. Lassiter contracted to do repair work at a cost of $300.00 in 1858.

ship[31] One year later, however, he was restored to the fellowship of the church and granted a license to preach the Gospel.[32] Upon the completion of several months of study in the theological department of Union University, Murfreesboro, Tennessee, Carter returned to his home toN. On June 30, 1861, he was "solemnly ordained to the work of the Gospel ministry" in a service held in the Murfreesboro Church, the ordaining presbytery consisting of McDowell, R. R. Overby, and A. M. Poindexter.[33]

The Civil Wars years were trying times for the church and for pastor McDowell. The financial situation grew bleak. As often happens in such crises, families were uprooted. The Negro members of the congregation eventually chose to establish independent churches of their own.[34] The Trustees of the Institute had left the management

---

[31] *Minutes*, January 1858.

[32] *Ibid.*, January 11, 1859; January 30, 1859.

[33] Joseph Ethelred Carter (1836-1889), who had prepared himself for the legal profession, spent the greater part of his relatively short ministry outside the bounds of North Carolina. He labored in Tennessee and Georgia during the early years of the Civil War. Returning to North Carolina, he preached in neighboring churches and conducted protracted meetings in the Roanoke-Chowan region during 1864-1865. In the latter year he settled in Danville, Kentucky, subsequently ministering to various churches in central Kentucky and serving as an Agent of the Southern Baptist Theological Seminary. He remained in Kentucky — except for a brief sojourn in Alabama and in Mississippi — until 1880. Returning again to North Carolina, Carter ministered to churches at Tarboro, Rocky Mount, Wilson, and Toisnot. In 1882 he moved to Hendersonville, where he served as pastor of the church there and became editor and proprietor of the *Western North Carolina Baptist*. He is buried in Riverside Cemetery in Murfreesboro.

A biographer (T. J. Taylor) spoke of Carter as a man of "rare intellectual gifts, a devout Christian, an able and successful minister, a loyal Baptist, who maintained the doctrine of God's word faithfully and fearlessly."

Joseph E. Carter was to remain the only "native son" who had prepared himself for the work of the Gospel ministry until John L. Whitley completed the divinity program at Southeastern Baptist Theological Seminary — 100 years after Carter had studied under J. M. Pendleton at Union. Whitley served as Minister of Christian Education with the Williamsburg (Virginia) Baptist Church, before accepting employment with the public schools in Virginia.

[34] The Murfreesboro Church never had a large number of Negro members.

of the school entirely in the hands of Hooper and McDowell in 1860, with McDowell assuming the presidency of the Institute upon Hooper's departure in 1861.[35] In 1866 McDowell resigned from the pastoral office, but his willingness to continue to serve "until another pastor can be secured" was an open invitation to the church to continue to elect him to that office.[36] Even after another pastor had been secured in 1873, McDowell was to enjoy only a brief respite from his labors. With his seemingly boundless energy and devotion, he probably would not have wanted it any other way.

In 1862, the church reported 12 "colored" members out of a total membership of 73. By 1866 there were only 2 Negro members remaining. Meherrin Church, on the other hand, reported 104 "colored" members in 1862, out of a membership of 317.

[35]The full account of Hooper's leaving Murfreesboro and the Chowan Baptist Female Institute is yet to be told, though it has been assumed that suspicions regarding his "pro-union" sentiments were the primary consideration. Technically, Hooper remained president of the Institute until the Trustees accepted his resignation in 1865. Even then, the Board of Trustees had such confidence in Hooper that they could: "*Resolve*, That this Board hold in grateful remembrance the invaluable services of Dr. Hooper, while acting as President of the Institute, and that it would be our pleasure, if we had the pecuniary ability, to urge his return and to maintain him in the presidency until the end of life."

[36]It must be recalled that the pastor of the church was elected annually for a 12-month period of service until the mid-1880s.

Chapter 3

Completing a Half-Century of Service, 1873-1898: The Pastorates of Mitchell, McDowell, Vann, Scarborough, Wood and Saunders

John Mitchell,[1] who succeeded McDowell in the pastorate, had been extended a call by the church as early as April 1872. He appears to have begun his services with the congregation in January 1873, with the report of a committee on securing a pastor noting that he had agreed to serve for 2 Sabbaths in each month.[2] His presence at church conference is first noted on April 26, 1873.

During the first year of Mitchell's pastorate the church moved to complement the diaconate with the election of L. D. L. Parker and G. D. Spiers to this position of honor and influence.[3] The process of

---

[1]John Mitchell (1826-1906) was a native of Bertie County and a graduate of Wake Forest College (1852). Already prominent among Baptists throughout the State, he had served as an Agent for Wake Forest College, had twice preached the Introductory Sermon before the annual sessions of the Baptist State Convention (1861, 1868), and had held pastorates in Hillsborough, Greensboro, and with several churches in the Chowan Association. He was later to serve the Convention as Secretary of its Education Board.

[2]*Minutes*, January 4, 1873. Mitchell also served the churches at Galatia and at Winton during the period of his first pastorate in Murfreesboro.

[3]L. D. L. Parker had joined the church by letter from Galatia Baptist

revising the church roll was undertaken by a duly appointed committee, consisting of James A. Delke,[4] L. T. Spiers, and Archibald McDowell. The final report of this committee was presented to conference and adopted on April 25, 1874. It was agreed that "the Clerk should record the revised list as submitted; but the names of those not known to be members shall not be counted in making reports of members."[5] Later in the same year Mitchell, McDowell, and Delke were authorized to revise the Articles of Faith, Covenant, and Rules of Decorum, with their revised statements accepted by the church in conference on October 24, 1874.[6]

Since the Covenant committed the membership to "attend our Church meetings . . . and not absent ourselves from the Communion of the Lord's Supper without a lawful excuse," renewed attention was given to the growing problem of absenteeism. In late 1875 the clerk was instructed to "report to next Conference the names of all male members who are habitually absent from Conference."[7] At the same time, the clerk was called upon to "prepare a schedule of all who do, and of all who do not, pay anything to the Church . . . ."[8]

Church membership had reached an all-time high of 107. The Sunday Schools — under the superintendency of McDowell and L. T.

Church in April 1870. He was dismissed by letter on March 4, 1877. Genie D. Spiers — son of B. A. Spiers — had been baptized by McDowell in 1867.

[4]James Almerius Delke (1821-1892), the son of the Reverend James Delke, was Professor of Mathematics, Natural Science, and Belles Lettres at Chowan, 1865-1881. He represented the church frequently in the annual meetings of the Chowan Association and the Bertie Union, and was an avid supporter of the Sunday School movement. He had also been instrumental in the founding of the Chowan Reynoldson Academy, and had ambitions for making it a college for men. The Association, however, refused to countenance or support such a move.

[5]Minutes, April 25, 1874.

[6]The Articles of Faith, Covenant, and Rules of Decorum found in Church Record Book I (and in Appendix A of this work) are these "revised" editions.

[7]Minutes, October 23, 1875. From January 1873-October 1875 the "call of the roll" noted an average of 12 absences on the part of male members at each conference. The church reported only 16 male members in 1873; 19 male members in 1874; and 26 male members in 1875.

[8]Ibid.

Spiers — reported an enrollment of 135 scholars, with an average attendance of 120.[9] Thus, it must have been painful to the church to have to hear and to accept Mitchell's resignation in October 1875, after almost 3 years of very acceptable and faithful service. The resolution passed in this regard expressed well the sentiments of the congregation: "Resolved: that in accepting the resignation of Rev. Jno. Mitchell of the pastorate of this Church we do so with unfeigned regret, and still [the] Church [entertains] the hope that he may, after a brief absence, feel it his duty to return and resume the position which he has filled so efficiently and satisfactory to us."[10]

But the church knew full well to whom she could turn until such time as that hope entertained with regard to Mitchell might be realized. Archibald McDowell had not ceased to be an industrious laborer in the church during his three-year respite from pastoral responsibilities. Thus, one may not be reading too much into the record if he sees joy and gratitude, mixed with an ever-so-slight "pang" of conscience, in the manner in which the church renewed her call to Elder McDowell:

Resolved, that we tender to Rev. A. McDowell the Pastorate of the Murfreesboro Baptist Church for the period of twelve months, beginning from the expiration of the term of its former Pastor.

Resolved: that, he receive as Compensation for his services a salary of two hundred and fifty dollars, for 2nd & 4th Sunday in each month.

Resolved further, that should his time and engagements permit him to preach oftener for us we will hold ourselves under renewed obligation for a continuation of gratuitous services, previously for many years, so generously rendered [italics mine].[11]

---

[9] Reports to the Chowan Association showed 2 schools being operated by the congregation, 1873-1881. One of these was being conducted on the premises of the Institute.

[10] *Minutes*, October 28, 1875.

[11] *Ibid.* This is the first mention of a specific salary to be paid McDowell. A "History of the Murfreesboro Baptist Church" — prepared in 1930 by

In January 1876 the deacons were given the responsibility of contacting the habitual absentees on behalf of the church. In a further effort to encourage pursuit of covenant vows, the clerk was instructed to write all non-residents who had been absent from conference for more than one year, suggesting the propriety of moving their church membership.[12] Four years later this list of "delinquents" had grown to a total of 43, with the clerk then instructed to send postal cards to each of these with regard to his membership status.[13]

Adequate finances — especially for incidental expenses and pastor's salary — continued to be a major concern throughout McDowell's second term as pastor of the church.[14] In addition, the building was in need of repairs which would incur fairly large expenditures.[15] An entry in the records of church conference in mid-1878 may be taken as indicative of the typical situation throughout the 1870s: "The Deacons now presented their financial report for the Quarter just past, which showed the financial department of the Church to be (in many respects) in a very sad and unhealthy condition and especially in regard to Pastor's salary, which was very much behind."[16]

But the healthy life of the church at worship and in Bible study continued apace. McDowell was conducting services on each Lord's

---

Herman H. Babb, Mrs. G. T. Underwood, and Mrs. E. B. Vaughan — indicates that McDowell's personal records reflected "salaries" from the church ranging from a high of $313.40 (in 1861-62) to a low of $11.00 (in 1870-71). These records had been provided by Eunice McDowell and Ruth McDowell Day.

[12]*Ibid.*, April 26, 1877.

[13]*Ibid.*, January 1880.

[14]Deficiencies in funds on hand were reported frequently. A closing financial report for the associational year 1877-78 noted $154.75 still due on pastor's salary.

[15]On January 22, 1876, conference heard a report indicating that $396.58 had been spent on repairs. Work done included repairs to the old vestibule, drilling a well and installing a new pump, and some exterior painting. Several years later the old vestibule was removed completely, altering significantly the exterior appearance of the building, as per Samuel Wheeler's earlier description.

[16]*Minutes*, July 15, 1878.

day, except on those occasions when a 5th Sunday occurred.[17] McDowell and Spiers continued to lead the Sunday Schools in their work. The most noteworthy protracted meeting since the days of Reynoldson occurred in June 1875, under the preaching of the Reverend F. M. Jordan.[18]

It must have been known, however, that McDowell preferred a change of pace as regards the demands being made upon his time and energies. Accordingly, an attempt to realize that hope expressed earlier for Mitchell's return had been made in October 1877 with the extension of a call to Mitchell for a "renewal of his former connection with the Church as Pastor."[19] In mid-1878 the call was extended, again, with the pledge of a salary of at least $300.00.[20] Finally, in November 1878 the church instructed the clerk to write Mitchell, stating the "many reasons why they thought he should resign his Pastorate in Asheville and return as Shepherd of the little flock in Murfreesboro."[21]

John Mitchell had returned to "shepherd the little flock" in Murfreesboro by January 1, 1880, when his presence is noted as moderator of church conference on that date. A total of $247.00 had been subscribed towards his promised salary of "$300.00 or more"

---

[17]The quarterly meetings of the Bertie Union occupied 5th Sundays.

[18]A stirring account of this series of meetings is found in Jordan's autobiography *Life and Labors of Elder F. M. Jordan*. The entry in his diary for Sunday, June 19 (a week after the meetings commenced), reads: "Nineteen received for baptism, thirteen young ladies of the C. B. F. Institute, and six young men. A great Meeting tonight; six professions of faith in Christ — don't think I ever witnessed a happier time. To-day dear little Anna Caswell, who has been an humble penitent all the Meeting, was sitting in the summer-house, reading her Bible, and there alone found Jesus precious to her soul, in the pardon of her sins. She has been the subject of many prayers — has no father or mother to pray for her. Thirteen young ladies united with the church to-day." Jordan baptized 32 persons at the close of the series of meetings, July 4, 1875.

[19]*Minutes*, October 27, 1887.

[20]*Ibid.*, August 22, 1878.

[21]Unfortunately, no copy of this letter is extant. Thus, one can only surmise the "many reasons" advanced by the church in behalf of Mitchell's return.

by the time of his return.[22] At first he preached for the congregation on four Sundays each month. But he was soon engaged for additional services by the Sandy Run and Bethlehem churches, necessitating a return to services twice each month with the Murfreesboro congregation.

On May 27, 1881, the church and the community were saddened at the news of the death of Archibald McDowell. He had quite literally "given" the congregation a large measure of his talents and energies over a period of 26 years. The sentiments of the congregation at his passing were expressed ably and eloquently in a series of resolutions authorized by the church in June 1881. The author was probably James A. Delke.

In Memoriam of Rev. A. McDowell

Whereas: Our Heavenly Father, about 5 O'Clock P.M. Friday May 27th 1881 was pleased "to take unto Himself" our revered friend and beloved brother, Rev. Archibald McDowell, D.D. thereby depriving this church of a wise counsellor, and earnest Colaborough (sic), and a noble pattern; And whereas, we, his survivors feeling conscious that he was invested with the sublime dignity of being able to clearly apprehend and earnestly aim at the perfections of the deity; that he was "no Vessel set afloat without chart or Pilot" but having his eye fixed steadily on the "Haven of Rest" and trusting implicitly in the "Captain of his salvation," he pressed vigorously, yet wisely on — seemingly to realize this truth: "Who so keepeth his mouth and his tongue, keepeth his soul from trouble." — Therefore:

Resolved 1st: that we bow in meak (sic) submission to that supreme Head of the Church, who in His own good time has transferred His faithful servant from the Church

---

[22]*Minutes*, January 1, 1880. It should not be gathered from these references to salary that Mitchell was likely to detain his return to Murfreesboro because of the inadequacy of the salary offered or actually given. On the contrary, Mitchell was a very liberal contributor to various benevolent causes — including the work of the Murfreesboro Church, the education of indigent students at Chowan, Wake Forest College, and the Thomasville Orphanage.

militant to the Church triumphant, and further, whilst we accept, unmumeringly (sic), this dispensation of an All wise Being, yet we do rejoice in that our beloved brother has left us such a rich legacy — HIS CHRISTIAN EXAMPLE.

Resolved 2nd: That, to the wife, thus bereft of a kind and affectionate husband, whose depth of sorrow none can fathom, and whose pangs of pain, no word can sooth (sic), we would say: Trust Him!

Resolved 3rd — That to the sons and daughters, thus bereft of a wise and considerate parent, whose example, both by word and deed, ever tended to point them to the lamb of God, we would say: FOLLOW HIM!

Resolved 4th — That a copy of these resolutions be sent to the members of the family, giving evidence of our grief in the death of Brother McDowell, and assuring them that his death is not only a loss to them, but also to the Church, the town, the Community, the County, the Commonwealth, and the world. It comforts us, however, to know, they sorrow not as those who have no hope, for "Earth has no sorrows that Heaven Can not Cure." Resolved 5th — That a copy of these resolutions be sent to the Biblical Recorder, Raleigh; Albemarle Enquirer, Murfreesboro, N.C.; Orphans Friend, Oxford; Roanoke Patron, Potecasi; and Economist, E. City, N.C. for publication.[23]

But the same conference which authorized the preparation of these resolutions in appreciation of the life and work of McDowell also took note of the recent services of a native son of Hertford County for his "earnest and zealous preaching, singing and praying with this church for several successive days just past; the result of which was the conversion of 25 & the restoration of 5 precious souls, and the baptism of 12 into the fellowship of this Church." The reference is to Richard Tilman Vann,[24] who was soon listed as Mitchell's

---

[23]Appended to the *Minutes* of Church Conference for June 1881.

[24]Richard Tilman Vann (1851-1941) was the son of Albert G. and Harriett (Gatling) Vann. He had graduated at the head of his class at Wake Forest in 1873 and had done graduate study at the Southern Baptist Theological

"assistant," and who was to become his successor.[25]

Mitchell and Vann continued to work together as pastor and assistant until the resignation of the former in November 1882. By January 1883 a committee reported that Vann had agreed to accept the full pastoral responsibilities of the church at a salary of $400.00, but only upon the mutual acceptance of certain conditions. "It must be remembered," Vann wrote in his letter of acceptance, "that my work at the Institute, so long as I am a member of its faculty, must take precedence of all other work: . . . As to services during vacations, I should be able to make no regular appointments with you; the most that I could promise [would] be to preach as often as I conveniently could."[26] The church found these conditions acceptable and called Vann to the pastorate.

Eight months later, Vann tendered his resignation, to be effective on October 1. Of particular interest during the months of his brief pastorate was a notable attempt to formulate a better system for the collecting of monies to be appropriated to the various benevolent objects of the denomination. A temporary measure — proposed by the deacons and adopted by the church — called for the designation of particular Sundays as the times at which the collection would be designated for specific objects.[27] In less than two years this procedure

---

Seminary, 1873-1875. Though he was to hold significant pastorates in Wake Forest, Edenton, and Scotland Neck, his primary service to the denomination was in the field of education. He taught at the Scotland Neck Academy (1877-1879), Chowan Baptist Female Institute (1881-1883), and was president of Meredith College (1900-1915). After leaving Meredith, he was closely identified with the Baptist State Convention until his death, serving as Secretary of Education and as Secretary of Benevolence and Ministerial Relief. Vann's attainments are all the more remarkable when it is remembered that he had lost both arms in a childhood accident!

[25]The *Minutes* of the Chowan Association for 1882 list Vann as "assistant" to Mitchell. He was preaching on 2nd & 4th Sundays, while Mitchell was engaged elsewhere.

[26]*Minutes*, January 17, 1883.

[27]*Ibid.*, April 1883. Collections received at Sunday evening services were to be designated as follows: January, May, and September collections to Foreign Missions; February, June, and October collections to State Missions; July and November collections to Home Missions; and April, August, and

would be enhanced further by the adoption of the "Envelope System."[28]

With Vann's departure, the church turned, again, to one who had recently joined the faculty of the Institute. This was C. W. Scarborough[29] — a man whose pastoral service to the congregation would also prove to be of short duration, but whose counsel and wisdom in the capacity of member and deacon remained available to the church for some 35 years.[30]

Scarborough's work as pastor would extend over a period of only eight months. In a letter read before church conference in September 1884, he wrote: "It is a matter of deep regret to me that duty looks in that direction [that is, resigning the pastoral care of the church]. I do so with sorrow that I have done so little for it, and with grateful remembrances of the Christian love shown me by the Church. I am ready to do all in my power to help in securing a

---

December collections to Education. 5th Sunday collections were to go to the Sunday School Board (State).

[28]*Ibid.*, February 1885. "It was ordered the collecting for the Boards through the Envelope System and Sisters Mittie Carter and Sallie C. White to keep the Book."

[29]Charles Wesley Scarborough (1847-1922) was an 1877 graduate of Wake Forest. He had come to Chowan in 1883 as Professor of English Literature and Moral Philosophy, after having served as an Instructor at Wake Forest and as pastor of churches in Wake County. Other pastorates in the West Chowan Association included the churches at Jackson, Sandy Run, Robert's Chapel, Aulander, Buckhorn, Hebron, Menola, Pleasant Grove, Woodland, and Mt. Tabor.

[30]Scarborough remained a member of the Murfreesboro Church, 1883-1909; 1912-1918. He taught at Chowan, 1883-1890, as did his second wife, Mattie Saltzman Scarborough. The church adopted the following statement at conference in June 1885: "Being informed that Bro. C. W. Scarborough was a Deacon before he joined us, and feeling our *very great need* and inability to fill the Office of Deacon & the necessity of his aid and Counsel in discharging the duties we owe to God, and the Church; and also feeling the great responsibility resting upon us for the faithful discharge of these duties; we do, in consideration of these reasons, and many others, move that, Bro. Scarborough be recognized or Elected Deacon tonight, and that he enter upon the duties of Deacon at once without further ordination."

Pastor."[31]

When T. G. Wood[32] succeeded Scarborough as pastor in January 1885, the primary responsibilities for leadership within the congregation had already begun to devolve upon men of a new generation. Leadership in the work of the Sunday School, vacated with the death of McDowell and the departure of Delke, was being handled ably by John B. Brewer,[33] McDowell's successor at the Institute. The work of the diaconate had been enhanced further by the "setting apart" of such men as G. W. Spencer, E. W. Nolley, H. H. Cooke, W. G. Freeman, Thomas A. Brett, and L. W. Bayley to this service.[34] David A. Day had been named assistant clerk in 1882.[35]

Wood may be credited with instilling a new sense of stewardship among the members of the church and congregation. Gifts to benevolences and to the "incidental expenses" of the church increased to the point that the West Chowan Association adopted a resolution to the effect that "the appropriation to the church at Murfreesboro ought to be discontinued."[36] The wisdom of carrying insurance on all church

---

[31]*Minutes,* September 1884. In this regard, the church gave Scarborough $18.20 in January 1885 "to pay in part his expenses in visiting Lawrenburg (sic), N.C., in securing the services of Bro. Wood who had already partially engaged his services with them as their Pastor for next year."

[32]Thomas Granbery Wood (1852-1914) was a native of Currituck County. He had attended Richmond College, and had been ordained by the Pleasant Grove Church (in Virginia-Portsmouth Association) in 1873. He was married to Isadora Askew, of Bertie County, an 1867 graduate of Chowan Female Institute. Wood served various churches in the Chowan and West Chowan associations in North Carolina and in the old Virginia-Portsmouth Association in Virginia.

[33]John Bruce Brewer (1846-1929) was president of the Chowan Female Institute, 1881-1896; 1918-1920. He served in the same capacity at Wilson Collegiate Institute, 1870-1876; Franklin Female Seminary, 1901-1907; and Roanoke College (now Averett), 1907-1918.

[34]Spencer and Nolley in 1876; Cooke and Freeman in 1878; Brett and Bayley in 1882.

[35]David A. Day (1855-1935) had recently settled in Murfreesboro, having married Ruth McDowell, 2nd daughter of Archibald and Mary McDowell. He was later to serve the church as a "collector" for pastor's salary and as a deacon.

[36]*Minutes of the Eleventh Annual Session of the West Chowan Baptist*

property gradually prevailed over the reservations and objections of some within the congregation.[37] Among the churches of the West Chowan Association, the Murfreesboro Church was reported number one in *per capita* giving in 1884, 1887, 1888-1891, and 1893.

The renewed emphasis on Temperance — prevalent throughout the nation — proved to be a major factor in the discipline exercised by the church.[38] But it was not only the members in covenant with God and one another who were called upon to rid themselves of the habit of imbibing in strong drink. In mid-1886 the clerk recorded: "The Church now voted to advocate, should it come up, the cause of removing the sale of Spirituous liquors from the town. . . ." But, as if to recognize the formidable nature of such a foe, it was added, "but at the same [time] could not see any possible chance of doing so; but resolved to *try*.[39]

Early in Wood's pastorate there is a reference to the work of a new organization within the church — an organization which was to

Association, Held With the Baptist Church at Coleraine, Bertie County, N.C., October 24, 25 and 26, 1893 (Raleigh: Edwards & Broughton, 1893), p. 6. The "appropriation" referred to appears to have been coming from the State Board of Missions. However, this is the only reference found to such an appropriation this early in the life of the church.

[37]In August 1885 it was ordered that "the Deacons constitute a committee to advise on the necessity of insuring the Church and report as early as possible." When the matter of insurance coverage continued to be delayed until February 1886, "a *few* of the members feeling more keenly the importance of the matter concluded that they would, at their own expense, take out a policy on same for $1000.00 at a cost of $12.50 in the name of the Pastor for the benefit of the entire Church."

[38]Wood was a strong advocate of total abstinence, both in the church and in the West Chowan Association. During the period of his pastorate the church excluded 2 persons for drunkenness, 1 for "sale of spirituous liquors," and 1 for "traffic in whiskey." On one occasion a brother — who had been cited to appear before the church — wrote a letter of apology for past drunkenness. The clerk was instructed to write the brother that "he would be forgiven by us if he would promise to entirely abstain from the use of strong and intoxicating drinks."

[39]*Minutes*, May 1886.

attain a prominence and a recognition previously denied to those who exercised its ministry. The reference reads:

> The Dorcas Society of the Murfreesboro Bap[tist] Church, with the hearty approval of the Entire Church (available) have purchased the adjoining lot, known as the M. W. Wise Lot, as a Parsonage for the use of the Murfreesboro Bap[tist] Church, at a total cost of $650.00. The society not having in hand the required funds, to settle off the same, applied to Dr. Jno. Mitchell, who kindly purchased the Lot for them in his own name, Executing to them a bond to make over the Lot to the Trustees of the Church whenever the purchase money shall have been paid.[40]

The church promptly acted to insure the lot in the amount of $500.00.

This "Dorcas Society," first noted in 1886, appears to have been the outgrowth of an earlier "Sewing Society," which had presented the church a gift of $300.00 as early as 1856.[41] The ladies of the church and congregation had taken a particular interest throughout the years in the provision of furnishings for the interior of the church building, and in keeping the grounds in good condition. Their primary source of funds was through the sale of handicrafts (quilts, embrodieries, etc.) of their own making. This first parsonage, purchased with the aid of John Mitchell, was to serve the church until it was sold to Isaac Pipkin in 1902.[42]

An early conterpart to the Dorcas Society was the Woman's Missionary Society. According to information gathered by Mrs. P. D. Sewell, and incorporated in her manuscript "History of Murfreesboro Baptist W. M. S." in 1939, the Woman's Missionary Society was organized in 1889 by a group of eight dedicated women of the church. These women were: Ruth McDowell Day, Anna Eldridge (later, Mrs.

---

[40] *Ibid.*, February 6, 1886.

[41] *Ibid.*, June 4, 1856.

[42] *Ibid.*, January 22, 1902. The price settled upon with Mr. Pipkin for the purchase of the lot was $125.00. The much-reduced price paid for the lot in 1902 — combined with a reference on December 10, 1896, to "cutting down trees killed by the fire on the church & parsonage lots"—makes it appear that this early parsonage must have been severely damaged, if not destroyed, by fire.

C. W. Scarborough), Lucy Boone Freeman, Ellen V. Carter, Ellen J. Sumner, Rockie DeLoatche, Dora Askew Wood, and Sylla Williamson. The group met, generally, in the home of Mrs. Day. The first president of the organization was Mrs. Day; the first secretary, Miss Eldridge.[43] Much more would be heard from this group of devoted women in later years.

But T. G. Wood — like each of his predecessors in the pastoral office — had a particular interest in and responsibility for the affairs of Chowan Baptist Female Institute. Thus, in 1888 Wood tendered his resignation as pastor of the Murfreesboro Church due to the time involved in his work as Agent for the Institute.[44] The church, however, refused to accept the resignation, urging Wood to "preach when he may be here; trying at least to give us two Sundays in the month."[45] In 1890 Wood asked for a "leave of absence for an indefinite time."[46] The church granted it. In the winter of 1893 Wood, again, tendered his resignation. A majority refused to accept it. This brought a response from Wood in the form of the following letter:

> I have received official notice, through brethren Spencer and Day, of your refusal to accept my resignation of recent date. This action of yours necessitates from me a formal reply. My resignation was due to a profound conviction that such a course would result in the greater harmony and efficiency of the Church. I still have the same conviction, and believe that it will be wisest and best for the church to release me and call to its pastorate some other man. At the same time, I am bound to respect the convictions of my brethren, and desire only to be guided by the Holy Spirit. Should the Church *unitedly* persist in the withdrawal of my resignation, and could honorable release be

---

[43]Much of the information for Mrs. Sewell's "History" is credited to the records and memory of Eunice McDowell, sister of Mrs. Day. The history was prepared for the 50th anniversary of the Ruth McDowell Day WMS. Mrs. Day had died in 1937.

[44]*Minutes*, May 3, 1888.

[45]*Ibid.*, May 6, 1888.

[46]*Ibid.*, June 26, 1890.

obtained from the other field, it would seem to be the Call of duty to remain. But such a course I cannot advise for the following reasons:

1st. It has the appearance of fickleness, and may react disastrously upon Church and pastor.

2nd. It may prove difficult of accomplishment, and require much time and effort.

3rd. My Convictions are against it.

Praying for you collectively and individually the blessings of Almighty God, and the guidance of the Holy Spirit I remain

Yours fraternally,

Thos. G. Wood

After "due consideration" the church finally voted to accept the resignation, 20-2.[47]

On December 24, 1893, a unanimous call was extended the Reverend Samuel Saunders,[48] "at a salary of $300 and a home free of charge, not including furniture."[49] Beginning his pastoral services in early February 1894, Saunders baptized 15 new converts on May 13 of the same year. Renewed efforts were made towards securing needed repairs to church properties.[50] Upon request of the new president of the Institute, W. O. Petty, Saunders was granted a release from his preaching duties during the summer months of 1896 in order to "canvas for the School at the Institute."[51] Further effort

---

[47] Ibid., December 3, 1893.

[48] Samuel Saunders (1842-1911?) was born in Northampton County, Virginia; had attended Richmond College and the Southern Baptist Theological Seminary. Ordained in 1871, he was serving the Baptist churches in Radford and Dublin, Virginia, at the time of his call to Murfreesboro. He also served the Mt. Tabor, Seaboard, Union, and Chowan churches during his brief stay in the West Chowan Association. Saunders concluded his ministerial labors among churches in his native Virginia.

[49] Minutes, December 24, 1893.

[50] Ibid., March 19, 1894; June 10, 1894. The matter of taking care of much-needed repairs, especially to the ceiling and roof of the building, had been delayed repeatedly. Contract was reported let for roof repairs on June 10, 1896, at a contract price of $144.41.

[51] Petty had been elected president of the Institute in June 1896, with

was made to deal with those who neglected the financial needs of the church.[52]

After a period of four years as pastor of the church, Samuel Saunders resigned on March 19, 1898, to accept the pastoral call of the Calvary Baptist Church, Portsmouth, Virginia.[53] The end of his tenure as pastor saw the church approaching the conclusion of a half-century of service. The original membership of 31 had grown to a total of 99. The Sunday School reported 85 scholars, with Thomas A. Brett as superintendent. The women of the church and congregation were exerting greater voice and influence in the church's affairs, and were receiving — however grudgingly — a new recognition and respect for their capabilities.

There is no record of a Golden Anniversary celebration. Had it occurred, however, few of those present on that November day in 1848 could have been present for such an occasion. The future of the church had passed, indeed, to a new generation.[54]

Saunders his "associate." Personal animosity between the two resulted, eventually, in Petty's leaving the Murfreesboro Church and resigning the presidency of the Institute. In granting a letter of dismission to Petty, the church made it clear that she was not passing judgment upon the merits of quarrels between the two men. At the same time, she expressed full confidence in the pastor.

[52] *Minutes*, March 9, 1897. At this conference it was "Resolved that from and after this date this Church will not grant letters of dismission to members who have not paid a reasonable sum into the treasury of this Church to bear the necessary expenses of the Church. The Church shall be the judge as to what is reasonably due from the members to the Church, and will judge each case on its own merits."

[53] *Ibid.*, March 19, 1898.

[54] The pastor and the deacons had been named to a committee to arrange for a "Roll-Call or Reunion" service to be conducted in the spring or summer of 1891 — probably in anticipation of the approaching 50th anniversary of the church *meeting* in Murfreesboro. The project was still being discussed in September 1891, at which time the matter was postponed indefinitely.

The only surviving "charter" member of the church appears to have been James H. Lassiter, who was residing in Henderson, North Carolina, in 1898.

Chapter 4

Towards a Diamond Anniversary, 1898-1923: The Pastorates of Harrill, Howell, Sherwood, Davis, Woodall, Keaton, and Whitley

On October 25, 1898, a presbytery was called by the Murfrees-boro Baptist Church for the purpose of ordaining a young man to the full work of the Gospel ministry, "that he may be prepared and equipped to do the Master's work whenever and wherever he may be called."[1] The young man was G. P. Harrill,[2] a licentiate from Forest City, North Carolina, who had been called as supply preacher for the congregation in July 1898. The call was made permanent by action of the church in conference on September 15.

Harrill's tenure of 4 ½ years was marked by a continuation of those earlier efforts to improve the financial condition of the church — or, rather, to impress the importance of financial support upon all the membership. Efforts were made towards augmenting the role played by music in the church's worship. Attention was given to the care and upkeep of the buildings and grounds. The women of the

---

[1]Quoting letter addressed to the presbytery by action of church conference, October 13, 1898.

[2]George Pinckney Harrill (1865-1931?) had graduated from Wake Forest College in 1889, and had engaged in educational work at Yadkin Valley Institute, Trap Hill, and Forest City prior to being called as "supply pastor" for the Murfreesboro and Chowan churches. He also served Mt. Tabor during his tenure in the West Chowan Association. Harrill later served various churches in the Liberty, Central, Roanoke, and Chowan associations.

church expanded their mission in the wake of the growing significance of "woman's work" in both the local association and the conventions with which the church was affiliated.

The amount of monies actually contributed for the various expenses and benevolences of the church remained stable throughout the period.[3] But the question of faithfulness to the convenant vow to "be ready to Contribute, according as God has prospered us, to the expenses of the Church and for the support of the ministry" continued to be raised. Thus, a committee was appointed in 1900 "to apportion and collect" from the male members the specified amounts due the treasurer for expenses.[4] Three months later, John C. Scarborough[5] offered — and the church adopted — the following motion: "That the Deacons of this Church be instructed to examine into the financial condition of the Church and to find out for the Church the members who are failing to help meet the expenses of the Church, and to report with regular Conference the names of such members, that they may be labored with and disciplined for such failure — if persisted in."[6]

Music had played a significant role in the life of the church at worship from the very beginning. The selection and use of a particular hymnal, the services of a choir, and the presence and use of an organ were noted in earlier years.[7] Serious consideration was given to the purchase of a new organ after 1899, when a committee of four women was named to solicit the funds to defray expenses for needed repairs to the old organ.[8] Shortly thereafter, a committee was authorized to purchase a supply of copies of "The Baptist Hymnal" sufficient for the use of the congregation.[9] Both projects ran into

---

[3]Associational records reported receipts for all causes as follows: $500.61 in 1899; $565.90 in 1900; $541.33 in 1901; and $515.42 in 1902.

[4]*Minutes*, October 18, 1900.

[5]John Catre Scarborough(1841-1917), older brother of C. W. Scarborough, was president of Chowan Baptist Female Institute, 1897-1909. He served the church as a deacon (1897-1911) and as clerk (1907-1911) before moving to Ahoskie to assume work as principal of the local high school.

[6]*Minutes*, January 16, 1901.

[7]*Ibid.*, June 11, 1848; February 6, 1851; June 4, 1856.

[8]*Ibid.*, April 26, 1899.

[9]*Ibid.*, September 7, 1899; September 21, 1899.

difficulty, however, before they were finally accomplished.[10]

The deacons, as trustees of the church property, began to exercise a more significant role in the care of the buildings and grounds. Thus, the "Board of Deacons" was given at least three specific assignments by the church regarding matters relating to church properties during Harrill's pastorate.[11] The members of the Ladies' Aid Society, however, continued to assume major responsibility for this function, with the Society's function later to be described as that of "aiding the church in improving the church building and grounds . . ."[12]

Associational reports on the work of the women in the churches first takes note of the "Murfreesboro Baptist Church Sunbeams" in 1898, when a contribution to missions from this organization was reported in the amount of $12.50. The church's letter to the West Chowan Association in 1901 noted 84 members of the Sunbeam Band, with Fannie Gary as president.[13] Undoubtedly, much of the "basket" and "envelope" collections designated by the church for various benevolent objects came from the hands and labor of women — young and old.[14]

Four months elapsed between the time of Harrill's departure

10The committee had collected $10.00 for repairs to the organ by June 1899, with this amount reported spent on the necessary repairs. When the church agreed to sell the old parsonage lot in 1901, it was specifically noted that the proceeds from such a sale were *not* to be used for the purchase of a new organ. When the church finally purchased a new organ in 1903, she had to do so by *borrowing* the necessary funds from the Woman's Aid Society.

The committee on purchase of hymnals was unable to make its purchase until after March 1900 due to a deficit in the funds needed for that project.

11*Minutes*, November 9, 1899; January 23, 1901; January 22, 1902. The members of the diaconate had been constituted "trustees" of the church on January 20,1886, during the much-delayed effort to secure a deed for the church property (the original one having been destroyed by fire). It became customary to refer to the diaconate as a "Board of Deacons" around the turn of the century.

12This description of the Ladies' (Woman's) Aid Society is found in the church's letter to the West Chowan Association in 1909.

13Letter transcribed in Church Record Book I, following the *Minutes* of conference for October 16, 1898.

14Earlier contributions for mission causes came through the Sunday

to serve a church in Thomasville, North Carolina, and the arrival of his successor, A. T. Howell.[15] The announcement was made in late April 1903 that the new pastor would soon take up residence in Murfreesboro. A committee was named to arrange for the transportation of Howell and his family to the Sewell House from any "point of landing." The members of the Woman's Aid Society were requested to help with the welcome and the arrangements to be made for the permanent accommodations for Howell and his family.[16]

Howell's pastorate was marked by continuing efforts towards repairs upon and new furnishings for the house of worship which had now served the congregation for well over a half-century. The Ladies' Aid Society (or Woman's Aid Society) played a particularly prominent role in these regards. The church's letters to the West Chowan Association noted contributions by the Society to "Building & Repairs" of $137.55 in 1906; $39.92, in 1907.[17] One year earlier, these ladies had been given permission to "reseat" the sanctuary and to replace the old wooden supports under the gallery.[18] As noted previously, the purchase of a new organ in 1903 had been made possible through a "loan" from the Ladies' Aid Society.[19]

The general condition of the building made it advisable to let contracts for painting both the interior and exterior woodwork, as well as the roof. With this work in mind, a committee was appointed to determine the cost of painting the building and the roof.[20] Though

---

School Missionary Societies. A missionary society had been organized among the girls at C. B. F. Institute in the early 1850s.

[15]Albert Thomas Howell (1864-1946) was a native of Gates County, and an 1888 graduate of Wake Forest. He had spent the greater portion of his ministry prior to coming to Murfreesboro among churches in the Dover and Blue Ridge (Va.) Baptist associations. Howell served as Professor of Bible and Moral Science at Chowan College, 1909-1912. The last twenty-five years of his ministry were spent among churches in piedmont South Carolina.

[16]*Minutes*, April 29, 1903.

[17]Letters appended to *Minutes*, September 26, 1906; September 15, 1907.

[18]*Minutes*, April 19, 1905.

[19]*Ibid.*, March 18, 1903.

[20]*Ibid.*, March 22, 1905; March 21, 1906.

the work had to be delayed for a time due to the unavailability of paint, conference received a report on December 20, 1905, that the interior paint work had been completed and paid for. The following week a contract was awarded for painting the exterior of the building at a cost of $80.00.[21] The job of painting the roof had been completed and paid for by the summer of 1906.[22]

Church membership reached a new high of 120 in 1904. The Sunday School — with Hartwell V. Scarborough now serving as superintendent — reported an enrollment of 151 in 1906, with average weekly attendance of 90. The Sunbeam Band attracted large numbers of girls and boys, affording them the opportunity for both mission study and involvement — especially through contributions for benevolent objects.[23]

Howell resigned as pastor of the church, effective with the completion of the services on the 4th Sunday in September, 1907. The effectiveness of his leadership and the esteem in which he was held by the congregation may be safely judged by the fact that he would be called 2 ½ years later to serve the church again as her pastor.[24]

John C. Scarborough, church clerk, notes that A. C. Sherwood[25] began his ministry with the Murfreesboro Church on March 8, 1908. Scarborough concludes his notation with the words: "We record

---

[21]*Ibid.*, December 27, 1906.

[22]According to the report of the treasurer for the 2nd quarter of 1906, found appended to *Minutes*, June 28, 1906.

[23]Membership in the Sunbeams was reported as 90 in 1903, with contributions of $15.78; 88 in 1904, with contributions of $26.28; and 84 in 1905, with contributions of $12.31. The totals probably include the membership of the WMS as well as Sunbeams.

[24]Upon his resignation, Howell continued to serve the Mt. Tabor Church and assumed, subsequently, the pastoral duties at Potecasi (1907), Hebron (1908), and Mars Hill (1909), before his return to Murfreesboro.

[25]Arthur Columbus Sherwood (1877-1946) had graduated from Wake Forest College in 1903 and was serving Brassfields Church in the Central Association at the time of his call to Murfreesboro. He was later to serve churches in the Western North Carolina, Robeson, and Union associations in North Carolina before concluding his pastoral labors with First Baptist Church, Erwin, Tennessee.

here the expression of a good hope that his pastorate may be long continued and abundant in blessings upon people and pastor.'[26]

But Scarborough's hope was not to be realized, at least in terms of Sherwood's tenure in the pastorate. He remained with the congregation for two years, serving during a portion of that time as an instructor in the Chowan Institute. His letter of resignation — received on December 29, 1909, but to be effective with the 4th Sunday in March 1910 — cited the church's need for "more service and better service than I can render in my present state of health.'[27]

The hope of being able to resume services on every Lord's day in the month — a situation which had not prevailed since the days of Mitchell and Vann — had been entertained by the church in late 1909. To accomplish this end, application had been made to the State Mission Board for an annual appropriation of $350.00 towards pastoral salary. The appeal to the Board was made "in view of the importance for preaching in this Church each Sunday morning and evening because of the religious needs of the young women of Chowan Baptist Female Institute.'[28] But the realization of this hope was to be delayed due to the inability of the church to settle upon a man who could give his full time to the Murfreesboro congregation.

A call had been extended to A. T. Howell on March 9, 1910, with the expectation that he would be able to gain release from his

---

[26]*Minutes*, March 8, 1908.

[27]*Ibid.*, December 29, 1909. James D. Bruner, President of Chowan College, had earlier cited Sherwood's health as sufficient reason for not calling him to serve the church on a full-time basis. After the church had extended a call to Sherwood for his full services on December 15, 1909 — but conditioned upon receipt of financial aid from the State Mission Board — Bruner had asked the church to appoint him a "committee of one' to look out for [a] pastor of the church, stating that Bro. Sherwood is not strong enough for the work as pastor of the church for every Sunday of his time and Teacher for the C. B. F. Institute for part of his time." See *Minutes*, December 22, 1909.

Sherwood had been, in fact, serving "full-time" in a pastoral capacity, since he preached for the Chowan Church on 1st and 3rd Sundays in each month.

[28]*Minutes*, December 15, 1909.

other pastoral responsibilities in order to serve the Murfreesboro congregation. But the anticipated arrangement failed to materialize. The call to Howell then embraced services on the 2nd and 4th Sunday mornings, and on every Sunday evening.[29] He resumed his pastoral duties with the church on the 2nd Sunday in April in 1910.

Howell's later pastorate was marked by a renewed effort to press for the financial support of the church on the part of *all* the membership. After all, this was expecting no more than each had freely covenanted to do upon his baptism and reception into the fellowship. In June 1910 the deacons were appointed to apportion the amount due for pastor's salary among the membership, with a view towards receiving monthly payments.[30] If successful, such a scheme would relieve the church of a perennial embarrassment — quarterly deficits in the amount due and expended for pastoral salary. Before the end of the year, however, the treasurer's statement showed a balance due the pastor of $103.48.[31]

In March 1911 the church withdrew fellowship from six of her members — 2 males and 4 females — charging them with "non-support and non-attendance."[32] Three additional persons were excluded in June 1911 for non-support and unworthy conduct, after each had been visited by a committee from the church.[33] In a further attempt to "clear the church roll" of the names of persons who were making no contribution to the fellowship, the clerk was instructed to write certain individuals in order to ascertain, if possible, "their reasons for not getting letters and joining churches of like faith and order."[34]

---

[29]*Ibid.*, March 9, 1910. Mt. Tabor, Potecasi, and Mars Hill would not release Howell from his commitments to them.

[30]*Ibid.*, June 22, 1910.

[31]Treasurer's quarterly report in *Ibid.*, December 21, 1910.

[32]*Ibid.*, March 28, 1911.

[33]*Ibid.*, June 22, 1911.

[34]*Ibid.*, March 28, 1911. The necessity for purchasing a new Church Book, in which the names of the members would be enrolled, probably added impetus to this attempt at "clearing the church roll."

The year 1911 saw the organization of the first Baptist Young Peoples' Union for the benefit of the youth of the church and congregation. At first the BYPU met in conjunction with the regular weekly prayer meeting, with the expectation noted that "we all should strive to make the meeting as interesting and profitable as possible, . . ."[35] The year also witnessed the first instance of the appointment by the church of a nominating committee on officers and teachers for the Sunday School. Whether further "grading" of the School was also attempted at this time is unclear, though it seems improbable from the records available.[36]

Howell tendered his resignation as pastor of the church on Sunday, May 26, 1912, stating that "it was final." Three days later a committee consisting of the deacons, Rentz Sewell, and J. D. Bruner was appointed "to look out for a Pastor and report to the church."[37] Three months later the church approved a plan of co-operation with Chowan College, whereby the church could be assured of a full-time ministry, with the college furnishing ½ of the salary required for the retention of a minister for his full time.[38]

Q. C. Davis[39] was the first minister to serve the church and the college under this plan of co-operation advanced by J. D. Bruner and

---

[35]*Ibid.*, July 1911. The BYPU does not appear to have become a separate and distinct organization prior to 1921.

[36]*Ibid.*, September 20, 1911. The only Sunday School teachers whose names are given in the records at this early date are James I. Griffin, teacher of the Baraca Class; J. D. Babb, teacher of the Bible Class; Eunice Day, teacher of the Philathea Class; and Mrs. James I. Griffin, teacher of the Infant Class. Associational records indicate that the Sunday School included 20 officers and teachers in 1911.

[37]*Ibid.*, May 29, 1912.

[38]*Ibid.*, August 20, 1912. This plan of co-operation called for the outlay of $800.00 for pastoral salary, with the college providing $400.00 of the total.

[39]Quinton Clarence Davis (1862-1926?) was a graduate of Richmond College and Crozer Theological Seminary. He was serving Cashie, Roquist, and Hillside churches in Bertie County at the time of his call to Murfreesboro. He later served First Baptist Church, Albemarle, for a number of years. He was the father of William Hersey Davis, noted Professor of New Testament Greek at the Southern Baptist Theological Seminary.

adopted by the church. He began his services in September 1912, continuing as pastor through December 1913. During the same period he served as Professor of Bible, Greek, and Philosophy at Chowan College. An able scholar and an eloquent speaker, Davis was especially popular with the student generation.[40]

Davis' successor in the Murfreesboro pastorate, the Reverend W. H. Woodall,[41] served the church and the college for a period of only eight months. Called in mid-January of 1914, Woodall appears to have begun his pastoral labors in February. His resignation was received by the church in September, to be effective on October 1.[42]

Two items of particular significance were noted during the brief period of Woodall's ministry, both of which were approved by the church in conference on March 27, 1914. In the first place, the deacons recommended the building of a new parsonage to replace the one which had been destroyed by fire several years earlier. In the second place, the clerk records: "Our Pastor sugested (sic) certain committees for the benefit of our church work, which system was on motion approved."[43] There is no further reference, however, as to the nature and function of these suggested committees.

Two events of significance had occurred by the time T. C. Keaton,[44] who had been called as pastor on January 28, 1915, made

---

[40]Nettie Owen Freeman, secretary of the associational WMU, writes of Davis' eloquence in her report to the West Chowan Association regarding the July 1910 meeting of the associational WMU: "Then the orator of the West Chowan Association, Rev. Q. C. Davis . . . in his inimitable style, held the large audience enthralled while he handled the subject of missions under the heads: (1) Our Obligation to Missions; (2) Our Present Opportunities, as only a master can."

[41]William Harston Woodall (1858-1920) was a native of Tennessee, a graduate of Arkansas Industrial University, and the Newton Theological Seminary. He had served churches in Georgia, New Hampshire, and in western North Carolina prior to his brief pastorate in Murfreesboro. His last years were spent in the Buncombe Association.

[42]*Minutes*, September 1914.

[43]*Ibid.*, March 27, 1914.

[44]Thomas Calvin Keaton (1882-1973) came to the pastorate of the Murfreesboro church from a similar ministry with the Salem Baptist Church, Winston-

his first appearance at conference in March 1915. First, the church had voted to purchase the old J. S. Lawrence place, then owned by C. W. Mitchell, to be used for a parsonage. A committee had been instructed to "buy said house & lot at the cost of twenty-four hundred dollars, and get the best terms possible on the purchase."[45] Second, the gas lights in the house of worship were soon to be replaced with electric light fixtures, for the building had been wired for electricity, at a cost of $25.00.[46]

Keaton placed a strong emphasis upon reaching more persons through the ministry of the Sunday School, and upon enlisting greater numbers of students from Chowan College in the larger fellowship of the church. A special committee — consisting of W. A. McGlohon, Brownie Trader, Pearla Watson, Naomi Wiggins, and Eva Boyette — was appointed, "whose duty it shall be to enlist the unenlisted in the Sunday School."[47] Keaton appears to have initiated the practice of permitting students to come "under the watchcare" of the church during their stay at school, without the expectation that these students would move their memberships from their home churches. At any rate, some 67 students were received under watchcare of the church in October 1915, no one of whom appears to have later joined the church upon receipt of a letter of dismission from another church of like faith and order.[48]

An important decission was reached in conference in November 1915. The church decided that the time had come to proceed with the building of a new house of worship. Accordingly, committees on building and on finance were authorized and appointed, with instructions to proceed with plans for undertaking a building project. The

---

Salem. He had been a student at Wake Forest (1905-06), and was to spend but one year at Southern Baptist Seminary before returning to the pastorate of the North Winston Baptist Church. He retired after having spent many years with North Winston and Temple Baptist Churches in Winston-Salem.

[45] *Minutes*, March 11, 1915.

[46] *Ibid.*, March 25, 1915.

[47] *Ibid.*, September 9, 1915.

[48] *Ibid.*, October 1, 1915. At the opening of the 1916-17 session of the college, an additional 28 students were received "under watchcare."

Building Committee consisted of W. E. Jenkins, Uriah Watson, W. A. McGlohon, G. E. Lineberry, and C. E. Boyette. The Committee on Finance was composed of Rentz Sewell, James I. Griffin, C. W. Scarborough, J. D. Babb, and Sister N. T. Wiggins.[49] One month later, plans had been drawn for the new church building, with church conference adopting the same, "subject to changes which the building committee might see fit to make."[50]

But early enthusiasm for a new house of worship apparently yielded to doubts and fears regarding the realization of such a project. These, in turn, produced dissension and conflict. A remaining debt of some $2,000.00 on the parsonage and lot probably served to discourage many from entering wholeheartedly into a building project. An attempt in early 1916 to reduce the indebtedness on the parsonage to $1,000.00 met with only moderate success.[51] Finally, the original building committee was discharged on October 5, 1916, with the pastor requested to "appoint a time for a special conference meeting to discuss the church building proposition."[52]

Keaton complied with the request of the church by appointing a new committee of three persons: W. E. Jenkins, C. K. Harvey, and James I. Griffin. A new committee on finance was appointed also, consisting of C. W. Scarborough, C. W. Gardner, and J. D. Babb. But action on the matter of proceeding with the actual building project continued to be delayed, while attention was directed towards reducing the parsonage debt and meeting commitments towards other objects.[53] In a further attempt to strengthen the financial condition of

---

49 *Ibid.*, November 26, 1915. The church hoped to finance a portion of the cost of construction through aid from the State Mission Board.

50 *Ibid.*, December 23, 1915.

51 The proposed scheme called for the selling of a portion of the church lot, and of a portion of the parsonage property.

52 *Minutes*, October 5, 1916. The original committee appears to have become hopelessly divided over questions of the location of the proposed building, the procedures for financing the construction, architectural style, etc.

53 These new committees also had their difficulties. C. K. Harvey asked to be excused from further service on the committee in April 1917. No "progress" report on the part of either committee is noted throughout the remainder of Keaton's pastorate.

the church, the pastor was authorized to appoint a new Committee on Apportionment. The church also voted to name a financial secretary to keep accurate records of all contributions to the various objects of benevolence and concern.[54]

Keaton resigned as pastor of the church before further progress could be made towards the proposed building project.[55] Finally, in December 1918 the church voted to "undertake to raise funds for the purpose of building a church sometime in the future." A committee was then appointed to "solicit funds from the membership of the church and any other who might want to give something."[56]

H. G. Bryant, who had been serving churches in the Flat River Association, was called to the aid of the Murfreesboro congregation while a pulpit committee sought a successor to Keaton. This committee, which had been appointed in mid-1918, was prepared to recommend a pastor to the church in early 1919. Accordingly, the church voted to extend a call to the Reverend J. W. Whitley,[57] at a salary of $800.00 per annum. Whitley began his ministry on May 7, 1919.[58]

Some of those dreams and ambitions for the church which had been entertained by Keaton and his predecessors reached a new measure of realization during the years of Whitley's pastorate. The mood of the times was one of great optimism. The call of the denomination was, "Advance!" Baptists in the West Chowan Associ

---

[54]*Minutes*, March 14, 1918.

[55]*Ibid.*, June 23, 1918. Keaton resigned with the intention of continuing his studies in seminary.

[56]*Ibid.*, December 28, 1918.

[57]Julius Wesley Whitley (1879-1950?) had assumed the pastoral charge of the Bethel, Mountain Creek, and Pleasant Hill churches (Green River Association) upon completion of his studies at Wake Forest College. He was also serving as principal of Round Hill Academy. At the time of his call to Murfreesboro he was pastor of the East Gastonia Baptist Church, Gastonia. He returned to Gastonia to serve the Loray Church until the time of his retirement from the active ministry. The arrangement with Chowan College called for Whitley's service as Dean of the College. This arrangement was soon terminated, due to personal conflicts between Whitley and President J. B. Brewer.

[58]*Minutes*, March 23, 1919.

ation — including those of the Murfreesboro Church — seemed ready and willing to heed that call. While total contributions by the Murfreesboro congregation had reached an all-time high of $3,037.32 in the associational year 1917-1918, these figures climbed to $13,995.59 by 1921-22.[59] Statistics for the West Chowan Association in 1922-23 indicated an 11% gain in total Sunday School enrollments over comparable figures for 1917-18. The Murfreesboro Church, on the other hand, posted a gain of 116% over the same period in Sunday School enrollment![60] The youth organizations under the auspices of Woman's Missionary Union, together with the BYPU, showed signs of increasing vitality.[61] Church membership reached a total of 175 in the associational year 1922-23 — an increase of 51% over comparable figures for the year 1917-18.

At a special conference in June 1920 the church voted to erect a new parsonage, to be built on a parcel of land at the corner of Seminary Avenue and Elm Street, which land the church could purchase for $2,000.[62] One-half year later, a committee which had been appointed to sell the old parsonage property reported its work

---

[59]Total contributions by the Murfreesboro Church were the largest reported by any church in the West Chowan Association in the years 1921, 1922, and 1923. The financial tables for the associational year 1922-23 record a grand total of contributions through the churches of $131,874.18. The comparable figure for 1917-18 had been $82,380.62.

[60]Sunday School enrolment was reported as 255 in 1923. It was 118 in 1918.

[61]Associational records note a Young Woman's Auxiliary in the Murfreesboro Church as early as 1917, with Rebecca Long as president. The Baptist Young Peoples' Union — with Hugh White, president, and a membership of 23 in 1920 — reported an enrolment of 45 in 1921, with both Senior and Junior unions.

Antoinette White (Mrs. G. R. Hollomon) recalls being taken by Whitley, along with Elizabeth Watson, to a State BYPU Convention in 1920. She notes: "This was quite an adventure for two teenagers in those days. Mr. Whitley had a black Ford sedan with glass windows that rolled up and down, which was something."

[62]*Minutes,* June 23, 1920. The location included the lots at the corner of College and High streets, now owned by Margaret Evans Honn and by J. M. Askew.

accomplished. The parsonage and lot had been sold to Fred Parker for the sum of $4,000. On recommendation of the Board of Deacons, a committee of five persons was then appointed, "with instructions to make plans for [*a*] new Pastorium and submit same to the Church for approval. In case plans are approved they are instructed to build in case it will not cost over four thousand dollars."[63] Two weeks later plans and specifications had been approved, with a building committee directed to "have the building put up, using their best judgment."[64]

By October 1921 the church seemed ready, again, to undertake her most ambitious project to date — the construction of the new and expanded house of worship. This time, the project was to be accomplished, though not without many further difficulties.[65] The references to the progress and completion of the new building which are to be found in the *Minutes* of Church Conference are supplemented by a lengthy account prepared by Whitley and J. D. Babb. The major portion of that account is recorded here.

The New Baptist Church[66]

From the day that our Pastor . . . took up the work . . . there was a gentle agitation for a new Church building. Mushrooms spring up overnight, but great church

---

[63]*Ibid.*, February 9, 1921. This committee was composed of E. B. Vaughan, C. W. Gardner, D. F. Payne, Mrs. Thomas B. Wynn, and Mrs. George T. Underwood.

[64]*Ibid.*, February 23, 1921.

[65]A major point of conflict was with regard to the location of the proposed building. A bare majority of those present and voting in a called conference on January 1, 1922, had voted to erect the proposed building adjacent to the parsonage lot. However, an attempt to make this vote "unanimous" failed to pass. The entire action of the conference of January 1 with regard to the building was rescinded by conference on January 4.

It was, then, determined to send a ballot to each member of the church for his vote on the location of the new building. As reported on Sunday, January 22, the vote of the membership was: "Old Stand, 98 votes; New Lot, 41 votes."

[66]This account is found appended to the *Minutes* of Conference after December 22, 1922, though the account is dated January 20, 1925. The *Minutes* for March 5, 1922, noted: "All matters relative to the Building of our New

building programs come about slowly. It was nearly three years before there was any real definite move towards building. In the early summer of 1922, the Church appointed a committee on Plans and Specifications . . . . They thoroughly went into the matter and recommended a plan to the Church. This tentative plan was strenuously opposed by a few members of the church and the Committee asked for more time. Again they made a canvass of the various styles of church architecture and consulted Dr. Chas. E. Maddry and Mr. E. L. Middleton getting their views of the matters. They made their report to the church recommending three plans, but advised the Church to adopt the one previously presented to the Church. This the Church did almost unanimously.

The Church in Jan. 1921 sold their old Pastor's Home and bought a lot on the corner of Seminary Avenue and Elm Street. This lot was bought with a view to building the new Pastor's home upon it and then later to errect (sic) the new church building on the corner just about even with the College gate. The College was asked to deed a corner of the Campus to the Church for the purpose of building the new house on said lot. The Trustees of the College voted to make the Church a deed in fee simple. It looked like the New Church would be bult upon this corner . . . .

The next move was to appoint a Building committee. The Church appointed such a Committee consisting of ten members — the Pastor being a member ex officio. The following constituted this Committee — Bro. E. B. Vaughan, chairman; and brethren J. D. Babb, W. A. McGlohon, C. E. Boyette, W. P. Futrell, Dr. L. M. Futrell, C. W. Gardner, O. A. Chitty; and sisters, Mrs. T. B. Wynn and Mrs. G. T.

Church is being kept in a separate Book by our sectary (sic) of the building Committee." The Church Record Book contains no references to actions in conferences between the dates of December 18, 1922 and January 7, 1925.

The figure on the contract price found in paragraph 3 ($24,   .) is incomplete in the original document.

Underwood. This Committee employed Mr. H. L. Cain of Richmond, Va., to make the plans and specifications. He was also employed to superintend the erection of the building. After the plans and specifications were made, bids were advertised for. On the day when the bids were opened, Mr. E. C. Smith of Franklin, Va., was found to be the successful bidder. Accordingly, he was awarded the contract. The amount of the contract was $24,   . The contract for the art glass was awarded to Payne's Studio, Inc., Patterson, N. J., for $900 delivered. The contract for the pews and other Church furniture was awarded to The American Seating Co., Chicago, Ill., for $1,600.

The old building was sold to Mr. John Chitty for for $80.00. It was removed in the summer of 1922. Actual work on the new building began in the first of July, 1922. The building was to be completed within six months . . . .

. . . .

A word should be said about the place of worship while the new building was under construction. The Church asked the Trustees of Chowan College for the privilege of using the College auditorium and four class rooms for Sunday purposes. This request was granted by the Trustees. For nearly nine months, the Church worshipped at the College. During this time, on invitation from the M. E. Church, the Church held union prayer service with them. The B. Y. P. U.'s and Sunbeams met in the lower room of the Masonic hall . . . .

A word should be said about financing the project. After all, this is the hardest of all the tasks connected with the building of a great building. After the plans had been ratified by the Church, the Committee started the canvass to see how much could be raised in the local congregation. They began in a Biblical way — they started with themselves. The Committee including the Pastor pledged $10,000.00 in their own meeting before asking any one else to pledge. Thus a worthy pace was set which assured victory in the end. A canvass was made and more than $19,000 was subscribed. The fall before at the annual meeting of the West Chowan Association, the Pastor acting under instruction from the Church asked the Association to endorse an application of $10,000.00 to the State Mission Board payable in five years, $2,000 per year, until paid. The application was passed by the Association and was carried up before the State Mission Board. They cut it to $6,000 payable $2,000 per year until paid. Likewise the Home Mission Board was asked for $6,000 in accordance with a promise it had made to the various state boards that it would put dollar for dollar with the State Mission Board in church building at any and all our colleges, denominational and State institutions. The application was made, but the Home Board has absolutely refused to put one cent into the building pleading poverty on the account of the failure of so many to pay their pledges to The 75 Million Campaign.

The Church had to borrow money to keep the building going. The Peoples Bank of Murfreesboro was very kind and considerate with the building Committee in this matter. But some arrangement had to be made to carry the long term papers. Bro. E. B. Vaughan came to the rescue and put up his own collateral in the form of deeds of trust and the Church was enabled to borrow the money from County Commissioners who loaned money of the Sinking Fund of the Road Bonds. Thus the money was provided for through the generosity of Bro. E. B. Vaughan and the kindness of the County Commissioners.

On the first day of August 1924, the Church owed $19,000 and the interest on $12,000 from the first of Feb. 1924. The church decided to take out $15,000 in the North Carolina Mutual Building and Loan Association. This we did beginning with August with the understanding that we were to have the money on Feb. 1st next. The plan was to pay the indebtedness down to that amount and put all the Church's indebtedness into the Building and Loan. This would release Bro. Vaughan's collateral. Before the first of Feb., Bro. Vaughan had passed away and when his will was read, it was found that he had given $3,000 more to the Church with the condition that the Church release his collateral.

A word should be said about the work of the good ladies of the church. They were always on the alert to see what they could do. They bought a New Perfection range for the Pastor's new home, had window shades put up, and mats on the stair way. When the New Church was nearing completion, they put down the carpet, buying the best grade they could get. Since that time they have completed the kitchen in the Church and furnished it with silverware, china, cooking vessels, tables for the dining room and kitchen, bought a range for their own kitchen in the Church, and their latest addition to their equipment is a nice silver plated Coffee Urn electrically heated. This work was almost exclusively done by the Ladies' Aid Society. All honor to those who led and those who were led in this work.

The New Building stands here as a monument to the leadership of the Pastor, Julius W. Whitley and those who were willing to be led by him in this great building enterprise. Earth will never know of all the sacrifices, heartaches, and anxious hours that were made, felt, and passed through by these servants of the Most High. Only heaven will reveal all they did and all they endured and bore. No one on earth will ever be able to tell of the good the building will be to the multitude of College students who may come and go in all the years before us, and all those who live in the town, and all those who worship here just for the week end. Heaven alone will be able to keep this record and make it known at the last day.

The congregation first gathered for worship in the new building on the last Sunday in April, 1923. The account of Whitley and Babb notes: "It was a Red Letter day in the history of the Church. Every one was delighted with the beauty and comfort of the new building. It has been the subject of quite a bit of praise of former students of the College and old friends who have moved away, and of a multitude of strangers who pass this way."

As if to share such a "red letter" occasion with the entire Baptist constituency of the region, the Murfreesboro Church hosted the annual meeting of the West Chowan Association, October 30 and 31, 1923. Within a month the church would reach her Diamond Anniversary as a colony of God's people called Baptists, worshiping in Murfreesboro. Perhaps there could have been no more fitting way to celebrate this milestone in her continuing life than to share with fellow Baptists of the Roanoke-Chowan region the comforts of a commodious meeting house, together with ". . . Christian hospitality manifested . . . in their open homes, and a bountiful well-prepared food supply spread for our comfort during this session of our Association."[67]

---

[67]From a resolution of appreciation proposed by J. W. Downey, and found in *Minutes of the Forty-First Annual Session of the West Chowan Baptist Association, Held With Murfreesboro Baptist Church, Hertford County October 30 and 31, 1923* (Goldsboro: Nash Brothers, 1923), p. 24. This was the first occasion on which the church had hosted an associational meeting. Since that date the church has been a co-host for meetings in 1957 and in 1967.

Chapter 5

Rounding Out a Century of Service, 1923-1948: The Pastorates of Burrell, Owen, Bunn, Nickens, and Jones

Julius W. Whitley remained with the Murfreesboro congregation for some fourteen months following that associational meeting in 1923, with the church continuing to experience growth in all phases of her work, including finances. His resignation was tendered to the congregation on January 7, 1925. One month later the pulpit committee was ready with a recommendation for a successor to Whitley noting that their man — if called — would be able to begin his services no later than May 1.[1]

Accepting the recommendation of her pulpit committee, the church extended a call to W. R. Burrell,[2] of Monroe, North Carolina. His first services with the congregation were conducted on Sunday, May 10, 1925. Two months later — and in view of the financial obligations facing the church and congregation — he led the church to authorize

---

[1]*Minutes,* February 18, 1925.

[2]William Richard Burrell (? -1946) was a graduate of the Royal Military School of Canada, the University of Seattle, and of McMaster University Divinity School. He was employed jointly by the church and Chowan College, serving the latter as Professor of Religious Instruction and New Testament Greek. His salary was to be $3,250.00, with the college paying $1,000.00 of this amount. In 1925-26 he served as Acting President of the college, following the illness of C. P. Weaver. The later years of his ministry were spent in Asheville and Williamston, prior to his retirement in Lake Worth, Florida.

the appointment of a standing committee on finance, to be composed of three men and two women.[3]

The church continued to demonstrate vitality throughout Burrell's seven-year pastorate, especially in her worship life and in the youth organizations. An unbiased observer credited Burrell with being the best preacher in the association.[4] The work of the Sunbeams and of the BYPU thrived under the able leadership of devoted women like Mrs. G. T. Underwood, Miss Grace Parker, and Mrs. E. W. Whitley.[5] Mrs. Burrell was instrumental in reviving the Young Woman's Auxiliary in 1925-26.[6] A unit of Girls' Auxiliary and of Royal Ambassadors was noted in the church's report to the West Chowan Association for 1925-26[7]

W. B. Edwards,[8] president of Chowan College, continued a tradition of the chief executive officer of the school serving as superintendent of the church's Sunday School.[9] Enrolment remained well above 200 throughout the period, with average attendance in excess

---

[3]*Minutes,* July 1, 1925. The names of these committee members are not recorded.

[4]C. M. Billings, Historian of the West Chowan Association, writing in 1932: "Our hearts are sad because of Dr. Burrell's going. He was our best preacher and our profoundest scholar."

[5]Mrs. Underwood is listed as Sunbeam Leader, 1920-1923; as BYPU Leader, 1924-1926; and as president of the WMS, 1927-1929. Miss Grace Parker worked with Sunbeams, 1925-1926; BYPU, 1926-1932; and was also Financial Secretary for the church. Mrs. Whitley was Sunbeam Leader, 1927-1932.

[6]An earlier organization had been reported to the association in 1916-1917.

[7]Neither GAs nor RAs survived at this early date.

[8]Ward Blowers Edwards (1885-1935), a native of New York, was a graduate of Wake Forest College and of Columbia University. He came to Chowan in 1924 as Professor of German, Latin, and Dean of the College. He was elected president in 1926, serving in that capacity until his death at the opening of the fall term in 1935. He served the church throughout his stay in Murfreesboro as a deacon, as well as being superintendent of the Sunday School.

[9]McDowell, Brewer, and Weaver had served previously in this capacity over a span of 24 years.

of 100 during each of the years of Burrell's ministry.[10] The first Daily Vacation Bible School — at least, the first reported to the Association — enrolled 120 scholars, with an average daily attendance of 118.[11]

But the optimism with which the church entered the post war era was to be tempered in the face of economic reversals, culminating in the Great Depression of the 1930s. Of primary concern to the church, of course, was the financing of that huge debt which had been incurred through the construction of a new house of worship. An indebtedness of $10,000.00 was reported in 1927. By 1932 that figure had been reduced by less than $1,100.00, with the indebtedness on church properties standing at a total of $8,974.00.[12] At the same time, the church was attempting desperately to keep faith with the denomination in support of benevolences, at home and abroad.[13]

Valiant and sacrificial efforts were made towards meeting obligations on the church's debt. The lot adjacent to the parsonage was sold to Edgar Brett in 1928, with the proceeds earmarked for the indebtedness.[14] In December 1930 an arrangement was made for re-financing the bulk of the indebtedness with Jefferson Standard Life Insurance Company through taking out life insurance policies in the amount of $10,000 on two members of the church — Jesse Sewell and Archie Parker.[15] An Every Member Canvas was conducted in 1931, with the clerk noting in her records: "Every member of the church, no matter how young, will be asked to contribute something, if it is only a penny a Sunday that will encourage systematic giving, and also make them feel that they are really taking a part

---

[10]An enrolment high of 270 was reported in 1928. The top average attendance of 235 was recorded in 1927.

[11]Daily Vacation Bible School may have been conducted earlier, though the first report to the West Chowan Association is not found until 1932.

[12]As reported to the West Chowan Association in October 1932.

[13]The current practice was to report annual pledges to the association for the various benevolent objects. Commitments to the Cooperative Program — initiated in 1925 — were just beginning to gain favor with the churches.

[14]*Minutes*, February 15, 1928. The lot was sold for $1,000.00.

[15]*Ibid.*, December 7, 1930.

in the church life."[16] One year earlier, an arrangement had been made with the Conway Church for dividing the services of Burrell, "until such time as the present financial depression shall have passed or during the pleasure of the churches."[17]

Burrell's last year with the congregation was an especially crucial year with regard to meeting financial obligations on the indebtedness. The budget which had been adopted for the year called for total expenditures of only $2,500.00.[18] In mid-May a special conference was called to consider "the means by which to raise the money to pay the premium on Jesse Sewell's life insurance policy."[19] One month later, conference heard a report that Burrell had been paid only $194.00 to date on his salary for the year.[20] But, a mid-summer payment was due on the church debt. Accordingly, a committee of six persons was authorized to make "an every member canvas of the church and state the condition of the church to its members and ask them to take part in the raising of the amount which is due July 1st, the amount being around $750.00."[21]

By the appointed time, this committee had accomplished the task assigned it, the necessary amount having been raised to meet the payment due on the church's debt. In addition to the members of the committee, the church records single out Mrs. Ella Pearce for her efforts in raising funds.[22] The account of the church conference on July 1 concludes with the words: "The members of the church and many people of the town gave to this most worthy cause very whole heartedly."[23]

---

[16]*Ibid.*, December 3, 1931.

[17]*Ibid.*, December 14, 1930. Burrell reduced his own salary, voluntarily, on at least two occasions during his pastorate.

[18]*Ibid.*, January 10, 1932.

[19]*Ibid.*, May 15, 1932. The amount due was $38.00. E. W. Whitley paid the premium, on promise that the church would repay him within a few weeks.

[20]Ibid., June 8, 1932.

[21]*Ibid.* This committee was composed of C. W. Gardner, Robert Britton, Mrs. G. R. Hollomon, Mrs. T. B. Wynn, Mrs. George T. Underwood, and Miss Grace Parker.

[22]*Ibid.*, July 1, 1932.

[23]*Ibid.*

An overriding concern during the one-year pastorate of J. C. Owen[24] and throughout the six years of the ministry of J. H. Bunn[25] remained that of liquidating the indebtedness on church properties. In the final analysis, it is the women of the church who must be credited with rescuing the congregation from despondency with regard to the debt, and — finally — with providing a way out of indebtedness. Mrs. G. R. Hollomon provides the following vivid account of the work of the women during these bleak days:

The 1929-1930 financial crash produced a great depression and the women were deeply concerned about the possibility of losing the new church and new parsonage. For some reason, there seems to have been a dearth of male leadership in the church at this time, but it was a "shining hour" for the women . . . . The Woman's Missionary Union assumed responsibility for paying the interest on the parsonage debt. Mrs. G. T. Underwood was Woman's Missionary Union treasurer at the time and her records show this. The Woman's Missionary Union and the Ladies Aid Society did everything imaginable to raise money. One farmer gave, and barbecued, a pig from which the ladies made sandwiches, and the teenagers were put on the streets to sell them. No one could ever forget Mrs. Ella Pearce presiding over her huge pan of chicken salad like a "queen in the counting house" as she doled out the serv-

[24]Jesse Coleman Owen (1870-1955) had entered upon missionary service in China, following his graduation from Wake Forest College in 1899. He remained in China until 1911, after which he served churches in western North Carolina for a time. He was the Corresponding Secretary-Treasurer of the Baptist Convention of New Mexico at the time of his call to Murfreesboro in April 1933. Owen later served churches in western North Carolina, and spent his retirement years in Florida, Washington, Virginia, and North Carolina.

[25]John Henry Bunn (1890-   ) assumed pastoral charge of the church in July 1935, coming from the pastorate of the Lawrenceville and Warfield (Va.) Baptist churches. He later served lengthy pastorates with First Baptist Church, Morehead City, and with Edgemont Baptist Church, Durham. Now retired, he makes his home in Goldsboro, North Carolina.

ings at a chicken salad supper. Mrs. Pearce was a faithful worker and a generous giver during these lean times. Then there was Mrs. Lois Wynn, Miss Grace Parker, and Mrs. G. T. Underwood who walked the streets from week to week trying to get enough money to pay the preacher. If a person had no money, they would take a few pounds of cotton or a few pounds of peanuts to convert to cash.

The roof on the parsonage was leaking and no one had the money to fix it, so Mrs. Edgar Brett solicited enough money and paint to have the job done.

About this time the Ladies' Aid merged with the Woman's Missionary Union. Naturally, the Woman's Missionary Union was strengthened in membership, so its first big project was to pay off the entire debt of the parsonage. This they did without help from any other organization.[26]

Meanwhile, the church entertained the hope of finding a new source of income for purposes of debt retirement in late 1933. This was through the promise of $600.00 from the General Board of the Baptist State Convention. Since the Home Mission Board had earlier pledged to match such funds from State agencies, the pastor was instructed to write Secretary Lawrence in this regard.[27] But a delay in the receipt of promised funds from the General Board — along with the failure to subscribe the proposed budget for 1934 — necessitated the further extension of notes past due.[28]

In December 1935 a plan was proposed for removing the burden of the church's obligations to the Jefferson Standard Life Insurance Company. Again, it was woman's ingenuity that made the plan possible. Mrs. Ella Pearce, now a member of the Finance Committee, had discovered an individual who was willing to loan the church the

---

[26]Quoted from manuscript materials prepared by Mrs. Hollomon in connection with the preparation of this account.

[27]*Minutes*, December 1933. There is no further reference to the matter of aid through the Home Mission Board. At the time the Board had made its pledge to match funds, the Home Mission Board was making gifts to churches for construction purposes. By 1933, however, this program had been replaced by the Church Loan Fund.

[28]*Ibid.*, December 24, 1933.

sum of $3,500.00. Mrs. Pearce, herself, would loan an additional $2,000.00. With the income expected from the General Board, the church would be in a position to liquidate her obligation to Jefferson Standard Life if she could raise an additional $800.00.[29] At the regular conference of the church on December 15, 1935, this plan was endorsed. Conference "voted unanimously to secure the loans, and send Sister Ella Pearce and Bro. Ola A. Chitty to Greensboro, N. C., and pay off the loan."[30]

But concern with meeting financial obligations during these rough days of the Depression Era was not permitted to quench the ardor for being about the church's major business of ministry and mission. Church membership had grown to 241 by 1939. Woman's Missionary Union, including the youth auxiliaries of the church, continued to attract both the younger members of the congregation and their elders for the task of mission.[31] The pastors and their wives provided ready encouragement and leadership, just as their predecessors had done in the years before them.[32] Heavy indebted-

---

[29] *Ibid.*, December 11, 1935. The party willing to loan $3,500.00 was Mrs. Zoe Moorman who, along with her husband, had moved to Murfreesboro to spend their "retirement years." The proposal was attractive because it removed the heavy interest obligation on the indebtedness.

[30] *Ibid.*, December 15, 1935. Mrs. Moorman's "note" gave her first mortgage on the church property, along with "security" provided by the following endorsers of the note: Mrs. Thomas B. Wynn, Mrs. Ella Pearce, Mrs. G. T. Underwood, Miss Brownie Trader, Miss Grace Parker, C. E. Boyette, D. F. Payne, J. D. Payne, C. W. Gardner, W. P. Futrell, Ola A. Chitty, and Mrs. G. R. Hollomon.

[31] Mrs. Ola A. Chitty served as WMS president, 1933-1938. BYPU — later BTU — leadership was furnished by Miss Grace Parker, who also assumed leadership of the YWA group after 1934. Mrs. E. W. Whitley continued to guide the Sunbeams throughout the period. GAs and RAs, which had encountered "survival" problems in earlier years, received new attention through the efforts of counselors like Margaret Payne, Mrs. J. D. White, Katherine Lois Martin, Mrs. Bynum H. Brown, and Ola A. Chitty.

[32] Mr. and Mrs. J. C. Owen showed a special concern with the work of all the youth organizations. Mrs. J. H. Bunn was instrumental in expanding the outlook and the outreach of Woman's Missionary Union.

ness "at home" was not allowed to diminish the church's commitment to missions "afar."[33]

The women of the church maintained their vision and set the pace in meeting obligations as these arose. Mrs. P. D. Sewell notes that the WMS gave $600.00 to missions — including Chowan College — in 1938, and that within a span of four years the organization had reduced the debt on the parsonage by $900.00.[34] The occasion of the celebration of the 50th anniversary of the Murfreesboro WMS found Mrs. Sewell writing a poetic tribute to Ruth McDowell Day (who had died in 1937, and for whom the local WMS group had then been named). Her words, though directed to the memory of Mrs. Day, might also serve to characterize many of those stalwart women who sought to match their vision with action on behalf of their Lord and His church.

In Memoriam

As we celebrate this Golden Anniversary
Our hearts with fervor glow,
To know that God has cast our lot
Where living waters flow.

She is gone from our midst,
The one who began this noble work.
Yet her great spirit hovers near,
And bids us ne'er a duty shirk.

In my minds eye I see her
Treading softly down the aisle.
Her gentle manner each one did stir,
And, too, that beaming smile.

---

[33]For example, the church and her organizations reported the following total gifts to missions (apart from "local work"), 1930-1939: $439.65 in 1930; $385.20 in 1931; $185.08 in 1832; $152.25 in 1933; $175.67 in 1934; $244.92 in 1935; $252.59 in 1936; $358.55 in 1937; $590.47 in 1938; and $323.19 in 1939. The greater portion of these monies came through the WMS and related auxiliaries.

[34]Found in "History of Murfreesboro W. M. S."

In memory of this blessed one
Who served her Master well,
And ne'er did think her task was done
Until His message she did tell:

We pledge anew to do our best,
To proclaim His word with greater zest.
And, then, when traveling days are o'er,
May we, with her, enter into eternal rest.[35]

It remained for Bunn's successor in the Murfreesboro pastorate — the Reverend P. B. Nickens[36] — to preside over the occasion commemorative of the liquidation of the indebtedness incurred in the 1920s. A grand occasion it was to be, for the church had determined to combine a service of dedication of the debt-free building with a centennial celebration.[37] Highlighting the event would be the public burning of the last notes of indebtedness. A participant prepared the following account of this grand event:

The Baptist Church of Murfreesboro, N. C., was dedicated on Sunday December 13, 1942. On the previous Sunday, Dec. 6, 1942, the last dollar of the indebtedness was raised by the members of the church. What a glorious hour it was when we realized that the church debt was paid. No longer would we be compelled to work burdened down by a huge load of debt. At last we had shaken off the shackles and our shoulders were free.

Thus it was that on the second Sunday in December 1942 the church was officially dedicated to the service of

---

35 *Ibid.*

36 Paul Burton Nickens (1913-   ) who had graduated from Wake Forest College in 1937, was serving the Ludford Memorial Baptist Church, Plymouth, North Carolina, at the time of his call to Murfreesboro. He returned to Ludford Memorial in 1944, where he continued as pastor — except for a brief period during his days at the Southeastern Baptist Seminary — until his retirement in 1971.

37 The year 1942 marked the one hundredth anniversary of the "setting

God and humanity. Two former pastors of the church were with us, and had prominent parts on the program. Dr. J. H. Bunn, Pastor of the First Baptist Church, Morehead City, N. C., delivered the address. His subject was *The Challenge of The Times*. He delivered an inspiring message, and challenged us to greater tasks in the future. Dr. W. R. Burrell, Pastor of the Williamston Baptist Church, preached the Dedicatory Sermon. Dr. Burrell used as his Scripture reading the first six verses of Revelation 21. This great man of God likewise brought an inspiring message, using as his subject *The Builder and His Workmen*. A letter was also read by the Pastor from Rev. J. W. Whitley, former pastor of the church, and the man under whose leadership the present beautiful building was erected.

Also on the program for the day was Pres. H. Haddon Dudley, President of Chowan College, and the present pastor of the church, Paul B. Nickens. Pres. Dudley offered the opening prayer, and Rev. Mr. Nickens offered the dedicatory prayer.

A great crowd of friends and members of the church was present, and everyone went away feeling that he had been inspired and lifted up by the entire service.

One of the outstanding parts of the service was the burning of the church note. In charge of this very impressive service were the following: C. E. Boyette, E. W. Whitley, Mrs. Ella Pearce, and Mrs. T. B. Wynn.

Now having dedicated our church to God and His work, we are thinking of the words of Paul — "Forgetting the things that are behind, and reaching forth unto those things which are before, I press toward the mark for the prize of the high calling of God in Christ Jesus."

Yes, it was a great day for all of us. Everyone who was on the program gave his very best. The music was wonderful, anthems being sung by both the senior and the junior

off" of a "branch" of the Meherrin Church for the convenience of those members living in the town of Murfreesboro.

choirs. The attention was excellent, and everyone was con-
cious of the deep spirituality of the entire service. A letter,
read by the pastor, from one of our members in the armed
forces, showed that even those boys who could not be with
us were thinking about the service. It was truly an hour of
worship that shall not be soon forgotten. Let us not forget
that this service was made possible through the goodness of
God, and through the loyal cooperation of all the members
and friends of the church.[38]

The church experienced significant growth during Nickens'
ministry with her. Total membership had reached 318 by October
1943. Woman's Missionary Union reported 109 members in her
several unit organizations in late 1941, with Mrs. C. C. Lawrence
serving as president. The Sunday School reported an average weekly
attendance of 100 in 1942; 126, in 1943. With indebtedness a thing
of the past, gifts to non-local missions increased from $498.63 in
1942 to $1,146.41 in 1943.[39]

But Nickens' ministry in Murfreesboro was soon cut short by
the call to a different kind of service. He announced his resignation
as pastor on June 20, 1943, to be effective on July 11, "having entered
the service of the Government as an Army Chaplain."[40] Reluctantly,
the church voted to accept the resignation, "hoping that when he
returned from the Army as a chaplain, that he would return to us
and finish his work."[41]

The first century of service of the Murfreesboro Baptist Church
as a duly constituted body — apart from the "branch" relationship
to Meherrin — was completed with the ministry of J. L. Jones,[42] who

---

[38]This account, written by P. B. Nickens, is found appended to the *Minutes*
of Church Conference, after October 25, 1942.

[39]All data in this paragraph are taken from the annual reports to the
West Chowan Baptist Association.

[40]*Minutes*, June 20, 1943.

[41]*Ibid.*

[42]Junius Linwood Jones (1896-1961) had attended Wake Forest College,
1916-1921. He was called to the Murfreesboro Church from the pastorates of
the Rose Hill and Kenansville churches (Eastern Association). The remaining

began his services on the first Sunday in December of 1943. Once more, the pastor and his wife assumed significant leadership roles in the life of the congregation. In addition to his regular pastoral responsibilities, Jones served as Director of the Training Union, 1944-1948. Mrs. Jones directed the church choir program.

Though the indebtedness on the church building had been paid, work remained to be done with regard to furnishings and fixtures adequate to the services of a growing congregation. Word was received in 1944 that through the estate of Mrs. W. B. Edwards, the church had been left a gift of $640.00 to be used as payment on the purchase of a pipe organ, to be a "W. B. Edwards Memorial."[43] In late 1945 the church authorized her Finance Committee to sign a contract for the building of a 2 manual Moeller organ, pending the acceptability of a definite price.[44]

In May 1944 the church voted to spend an additional $2,000.00 on repairs and fixtures.[45] In September 1946 pews were ordered for the side alcoves to the main sanctuary, replacing the moveable chairs which had been used in these areas in former years.[46] In late 1947 the church purchased and installed a new hot air furnace at a cost of some $3,900.00.[47]

Paul Nickens did not return to the pastorate of the Murfreesboro Church, but he did return for a series of meetings in the fall of 1947. Attendance upon these meetings was reported as "very large." By the conclusion of the services, 32 persons had been received as candidates for membership in the church. It had truly been a season of revival.[48]

---

days of his ministry after leaving Murfreesboro were spent among churches in the Johnston and Robeson associations.

[43] *Minutes*, February 20, 1944.

[44] *Ibid.*, December 16, 1945. The church later voted to purchase a less expensive Hammond electric organ, rather than the Moeller.

[45] *Ibid.*, May 21, 1944.

[46] *Ibid.*, September 22, 1946.

[47] *Ibid.*, September 28, 1947.

[48] *Ibid.*, October 12, 1947. The scheduling of an annual "revival" meeting had been customary since the early days of the twentieth century. "Revival" meetings or "protracted" meetings were not as frequent prior to that time.

Jones tendered his resignation as pastor in October 1947, with the indication that it was to be effective on January 31, 1948.[49] By the time his successor had been called to the pastorate and had entered upon his labors, the church was approaching her 100th birthday. There would be no celebration of this occasion, however, for the Centennial had been celebrated six years earlier in connection with the dedication of the debt-free house of worship.

The church had also begun to schedule pre-Easter meetings during the ministry of J. H. Bunn.

Chapter 6

A Century and a Quarter, 1948-1973: The Pastorates of Taylor, Pruette, and Caulkins

Warren F. Taylor,[1] who had been called to succeed J. L. Jones as pastor in March 1948, began his ministry with the church in the early summer.[2] It was to be a ministry of eight years' duration, during which the church experienced as spectacular a growth as she had known over any other comparable span of time. Membership increased from 395 in 1948 to 475 in 1956. Woman's Missionary Union, which had reported an enrolment of 147 in eight unit auxiliaries in 1948, reported an enrolment of 190 in ten unit organizations in 1956.[3] The Sunday School reached a new high in enrolment in 1955, reporting 391 enrolled with an average attendance per Sunday of 230.[4] Baptist

---

[1]Warren Francis Taylor (1914-   ), a native of Washington, D. C., had graduated from Mars Hill College, Richmond College, and Crozer Theological Seminary. He was serving as pastor of the First Baptist Church, New Martinsville, West Virginia, at the time of his call to the Murfreesboro pastorate. He moved from Murfreesboro to the pastorate of Smithfield Baptist Church, Smithfield, Virginia.

[2]Taylor first appears as moderator of church conference in August 1948. He began his pastoral duties in July, after having been called to the Church on March 16, 1948.

[3]In 1948 the WMU reported the following enrolments: 80 in WMS, 12 in YWA, 25 in GA, 7 in RA, and 23 in Sunbeams. The 1956 figures were: 109 in WMS, 10 in YWA, 35 in GA, and 36 in Sunbeams. There was no functioning RA chapter.

[4]The previous high in average attendance was 235, reported in 1926-27.

Training Union reported an enrolment of 64 in 1955-56, with an average attendance of 46 each Sunday evening.[5]

The growth of the church at worship and in study necessitated the provision of expanded physical facilities. The annual letter to the West Chowan Association for 1951 noted that additional Sunday School quarters were then under construction.[6] But the congregation was also busy at the business of making the existing facilities more attractive and convenient. Thus, a committee was appointed in early 1949 "to beautify" the interior of the sanctuary.[7] By the end of the year, the church could report having spent a total of $4,000.00 for carpeting and interior paint work. An additional $12,000.00 had been spent in renovating the parsonage.[8]

The Woman's Missionary Society of the Church was rated A-1 in 1949. The Society had contributed $200.00 towards the furnishing of a dormitory room in the newly reopened Chowan College. The Murfreesboro unit had joined like organizations from other churches in Hertford County in the pledging of an annual scholarship for a needy student at the college.[9] Prior to the transfer of the responsibility for Royal Ambassadors from the WMU to the Baptist Brotherhood, the Murfreesboro unit had aided the pastor in a renewed ministry with the RAs.[10]

Taylor's resignation was read to the congregation on March 25, 1956.[11] At the same meeting which heard his resignation, the church approved a recommendation calling for the building of a new parsonage, on a site to be selected.[12] By the time a new pastor had arrived, general plans and specifications for the new parsonage had been approved.[13]

---

[5]BTU enrolment had reached a high of 93 in 1938-39.

[6]This construction refers to the educational unit at the north end of the present sanctuary.

[7]*Minutes,* January 30, 1949.

[8]In church's letter to the West Chowan Baptist Association.

[9]Data taken from manuscript materials compiled by Mrs. G. R. Hollomon.

[10]*Ibid.*

[11]*Minutes,* March 25, 1956.

[12]*Ibid.*

[13]The decision to build a new parsonage did not meet with the unanimous

The Reverend Rowland S. Pruette,[14] who was then serving as pastor of the Baptist Church at Cullowhee and as the Director of Baptist Student Union work at Western Carolina College, preached before the Murfreesboro congregation on Sunday, June 24, 1956. Having been the choice of the pulpit committee to assume the pastoral office vacated by Taylor, he was elected, unanimously, following the Sunday morning worship service at which he had preached.[15] He was to lead the congregation as pastor for a period of almost twelve years.

Pruette began his ministry in mid-August of 1956. By October 30 a contract had been awarded for the construction of the new parsonage. Conference had heard a report earlier in the month to the effect that the old parsonage had been sold to John McCready for $8,500.00 — a figure considerably lower than had been anticipated a few months earlier.[16] But within four years the Church had reduced the indebtedness on the new parsonage to a minimal amount, and had completed a major remodeling project within the sanctuary of the church building.[17]

Church membership during Pruette's tenure in the pastorate

---

approval of the Church. Some suggested spending up to $10,000.00 on further renovations to the existing home. Among those who cautioned against incurring further debt for a new parsonage were certain of the women of the congregation who had struggled to pay for the old one!

[14]Rowland Shaw Pruette, Jr. (1921-   ), a 1943 graduate of Wake Forest College, received the B. D. degree from Duke Divinity School in 1950. He had served as pastor of the Boonville Baptist Church (Yadkin Association) prior to assuming the dual role of pastor/student director at Cullowhee. He now serves on the faculty of Chowan College.

[15]*Minutes*, June 24, 1956.

[16]*Ibid.*, October 3, 1956. At the time the decision was made to build a new parsonage, it was anticipated that a minimum ov $10,000.00 could be received from the sale of the old one.

[17]A service of dedication was held on the first Sunday in August 1960. Remodeling involved the removal of the choir loft from the balcony level of the sanctuary to its present level, the building of a new baptistery, the installing of permanent pews in the balcony, the installation of the present wood paneling to the sides and rear of the choir loft, and the replacement of the central lighting fixtures.

increased by over 200, to a total of 683 in 1968.[18] Sunday School and Baptist Training Union reached new peak enrolments of 476 and 107, respectively.[19] The Church employed her first youth director in 1962, with John L. Whitley serving in this capacity[20]. Gifts to missions (non-local) passed the $10,000-mark for the first time in 1962-63.[21] Woman's Missionary Union had reached a peak enrolment of 244 in 1959-60, with a total of 15 unit organizations.[22]

During the associational year 1961-62 a new kind of ministry was initiated — a ministry which has continued to the present. Mrs. Edgar V. McKnight and Mrs. J. T. Johnson began the operation of a kindergarten program, making use of the educational facilities in the church building for this purpose. Twenty youngsters were enrolled in the program during that first year. Since that date the kindergarten program has been continued under the general supervision and auspices of a kindergarten committee, and with a staff of both qualified and dedicated teachers.

While the earlier renovations to the sanctuary provided additional space for the congregation at worship, it also displaced some of the Sunday School classes which had previously met in the balcony areas of the sanctuary. The educational unit which had been completed in 1952 was now being "cramped" to accommodate weekly Sunday School attendance in excess of 200 persons in 1964-65.

---

[18]Non-resident members, included.

[19]The highest average attendance ever reported in the Sunday School was 244 in 1960-61. Though Baptist Training Union reached a peak enrolment of 107 in 1958-59, the highest average weekly attendance (65) was recorded in 1962-63. Bob F. Hill served as the superintendent of the Sunday School, 1951-1957; and 1960-1967. Frances White was Baptist Training Union Director, 1956-1960. Others serving in this capacity after 1960 were Virginia James, John Prince, and Hargus Taylor.

[20]Whitley, a student at Southeastern Baptist Seminary, was employed jointly by the Murfreesboro Church and Chowan College for a weekend ministry. He served as Assistant to the Chaplain at Chowan.

[21]Total mission expenditures were reported as $11,915.00, of which $7,297.00 was channeled through the Cooperative Program.

[22]Mrs. John C. Gill was WMU president. There were 3 Sunbeam units, 3 GA units, 1 YWA unit, and 8 WMS "circles."

Accordingly, the Church purchased the Melvin Vinson property in 1965, with plans to convert the house into classrooms for the youth departments.[23] The Doris Chitty house and property had already been purchased in 1962 at a cost of $4,250.00, the property being converted into a much-needed parking lot.[24]

Woman's Missionary Union continued to foster programs of mission study, mission giving, and mission action throughout the period, though the number of women and girls actively engaged in the work of the organization had begun a decline from its peak enrolment in 1959-60.[25] The interests of both home and foreign missions were heralded through the "special" Annie Armstrong and Lottie Moon offerings, as well as through the championing of the Cooperative Program as the best method for supporting the total mission endeavors of the church and denomination.[26] With the Chowan College development campaign of 1957, Woman's Missionary Union pledged $1,000.00 — payable at the rate of $200.00 per year over a period of five years.[27]

Pruette, who had been doing occasional part-time teaching in the Department of Religion at Chowan College, yielded to the call of the college classroom in 1968. His resignation as pastor of the church was read before quarterly conference on January 17, with the indication that it would be effective as of June 30.[28] A pulpit committee, chaired by Ben Sutton, began at once the process of searching for the

---

[23] *Minutes,* October 5, 1965. Purchase price was $23,400.00.

[24] *Ibid.,* February 28, 1962.

[25] Enrolment figures noted: 236 in 1961; 191 (?) in 1962; 199 in 1963; 233 in 1964; 196 in 1965; 192 in 1966; 170 in 1967; and 165 in 1968.

[26] Mrs. G. R. Hollomon notes that WMU had given $59.35 to the Lottie Moon Offering as early as 1939. By 1968 this special offering for foreign missions exceeded $1,280.00. WMU established a goal of $410.00 for the Annie Armstrong Offering in 1967.

[27] Woman's Missionary Union — along with the church in general — has always been a strong supporter of Chowan College, whether in terms of scholarship programs, capital needs, or undesignated gifts to the operating fund. At present the church's budget calls for an annual expenditure of $500.00 for the college's operating fund; $900.00 for the development fund.

[28] *Minutes,* January 17, 1968.

right man "to go in and out and minister among us" — as an earlier generation would have expressed it — hoping to be able to settle upon a pastor without experiencing too long an "interim" following Pruette's departure date.

The man receiving the unanimous recommendation of the church's pulpit committee was the Reverend Thomas H. Caulkins,[29] then pastor of the Madison Avenue Baptist Church, Goldsboro, North Carolina. Caulkins began his ministerial labors on the first Sunday in August of 1968, having received the unanimous call of the Church in conference assembled.

Caulkins' ministry finds the church on the threshold of moving into the second quarter of her second century of service to the Baptists of Murfreesboro and vicinity. A new peak in total church membership was reached in 1970, when the annual report to the West Chowan Association noted a membership of 702. A new record was reached in total gifts for all purposes in 1971-72, when the letter to the West Chowan Baptist Association noted "total receipts" of $58,946.00 — the second highest total among the 60 churches comprising the association. Of these receipts, a total of $15,349.00 was labeled "mission expenditures," with $10,800.00 designated for Cooperative Program causes.[30]

In keeping with a general denominational trend, most of the church's "organizations" appear to be either stabilizing or declining in enrolment/participation over the last few years. Woman's Missionary Union reported an enrolment of only 131 in 1972, with a total

[29]Thomas Herbert Caulkins (1928-   ), a graduate of the University of Richmond and of Crozer Theological Seminary, had previously served churches in the Blackwater and Dan River associations in Virginia. He had served as pastor of the Madison Avenue Church for 5 years at the time of his call to the Murfreesboro pastorate.

[30]All records are taken from annual reports to the West Chowan Association. It should be noted that there are significant "gaps" in available church records for the years 1948-1973. Church Record Book II concludes with the Minutes of Church Conference for September 17, 1950. Following that date, the author could find no further records before March 1956. Only occasional conference records have been preserved for the years 1957-1969.

of 6 unit organizations.[31] With the demise of a general BTU program, the attempt was made to maintain a supper/forum meeting on Sunday evenings for the college students.[32] Average weekly attendance in the Sunday School has remained relatively stable over the last five years.[33] At the same time, Woman's Missionary Union has attempted to become more "interest centered" — again, in keeping with a denominational emphasis — by providing for "Bible Study" groups as well as for "Mission Action" groups. The music ministry is experiencing continuing interest/participation on the part of children and youth, but with a corresponding decline of interest/participation on the part of adults.[34] This, too, is in keeping with a general denominnational trend.

The Church was "debt-free" at the end of 1972.

A century and a quarter have come and gone since that little band of 31 souls united in faith and covenant to be the Baptist Church of Jesus Christ, worshiping in Murfreesboro. Much has been accomplished throughout these years "in service to God and humanity."

---

[31]The 60 churches of the West Chowan Baptist Association reported 4810 persons enrolled in the various unit organizations of WMU in 1960. The comparable figure for 1972 was 2984.

[32]Again, Baptist Training Union was a functioning organization in 33 of the 60 churches of the West Chowan Association in 1960. Only 16 churches — including Murfreesboro Baptist Church — reported conducting a Training Union ministry in 1972.

[33]Average Sunday School attendance for the Murfreesboro Church has been as follows over the last five years: 200 in 1967-68; 190 in 1968-69; 200 in 1969-70; 180 in 1970-71; and 190 in 1971-72. Current figures for 1972-73 are "below" the 1971-72 totals.

[34]In 1968 there were 50 persons enrolled in youth choirs, 25 in adult choir. In 1972 there were 45 in youth choirs, and 14 in the adult choir. Little has been noted regarding the on-going music ministry of the Church throughout the years. Among those who have served as organist/pianist or as music director have been: Sylla Williamson, Helen Watson, Ethel Boyette, Fannie Boyette Underwood, Mrs. R. R. McCulloch, Joel C. Holland, Violet Holland, James Brisson, Alton Parker, Betty Chitty, Mrs. J. L. Jones, Helen Baumgartner, Paul Baumgartner, Rose G. Pool, Anna Belle Crouch, Robert G. Mulder, Louise Griffin, and James M. Chamblee. There are undoubtedly others whose names have not been recorded in the official church records.

As Paul B. Nicken expressed it in 1942. It is hoped that this account of the past may provide added stimulus to the Church of the presen towards meeting the future "in faith and covenant" with God, and with one another.

Articles of Faith,
Church Covenant,
Rules of Decorum

ARTICLES OF FAITH[1]

Art. 1st. We believe in the divine inspiration of the Old and New Testament, as the Complete and only infalible (sic) rule of faith and practice, which teaches us to believe in the being of one true and living God, and that there are three persons in the Godhead: To wit: Father, Son and Holy Ghost.

Art. 2nd. We believe in the fall of Man, the Corruption of human nature and the impotence of Man, whereby he was rendered totally unable to do that which is truly, properly, and spiritually good.

Art. 3rd. We believe in the electing love of God, the everlasting Covenant of grace, the particular redemption of man and that justification is by the imputed righteousness of God.

---

[1]These "revised" Articles of Faith were drawn up in 1874 by a committee consisting of John Mitchell, Archibald McDowell, and James A. Delke. The original Articles of Faith — adopted on November 16, 1848 — were those drawn up by a convention meeting in Woodville (Bertie County) in June 1848, and later adopted by the Chowan Association. The Woodville document was, in essence, the New Hampshire Confession of Faith.

These "revised" Articles are, in fact, the Articles of Faith of the

Art. 4th. We believe that pardon and reconciliation are through and by the precious blood of Jesus Christ, and that regeneration and justification are by the influences and operations of the Holy and divine Spirit.

Art. 5th. We believe in the final perseverence of the saints in grace: Viz. Being once truly and evangelically Converted, they will never finally fall away.

Art. 6th We believe in the resurrection of the dead, a final Judgement and that the happiness of the righteous and the torments of the wicked are alike interminable.

Art. 7th. We believe in the ordinance of baptism by immersion, that this is the only mode, and believers the only subjects of the ordinance; and that no person has a right to administer the ordinance, but those who have been Called of God, and regularly set apart to the work of the Ministry by the imposition of the hands of a Presbytery.

Art. 8th. We believe that the Lord's Supper is a Church Ordinance and that it is the indispensible (sic) duty of members to participate in said Ordinance.

Art. 9th. We believe that no person has a right to a good hope in Christ, whose deportment is inconsistent with his or her profession.

CHURCH COVENANT[2]

For as much as Almighty God, by His grace, has been pleased to Call us out of darkness into His marvelous light, and all of us having been

---

Meherrin Baptist Church, as found in Wheeler's *History*, and probably represent a rather standardized confession of faith.

[2]This Church Covenant is the covenant of the Meherrin Baptist Church. By the mid-nineteenth century it, too, had become a rather standard formula for churches of the Regular Baptist order.

regularly baptized upon a profession of faith in Christ Jesus, and having united ourselves to the Lord, and to one another in a gospel Church to be governed and guided by a discipline agreeable to the word of God, we do, therefore, in the name of our Lord Jesus, Covenant and agree, by His assistance, to maintain the discipline of the Church in brotherly love, while we endeavor faithfully to observe the following rules:

First: In brotherly love to pray for each other, to watch over one another, and if we discover anything amiss in any brother to go and tell him his fault according to the direction given by our Lord, Matt. 18. We also agree with God's assistance to pray in our families, attend our Church meetings, Observe the Lord's day and keep it holy, and not absent ourselves from the Communion of the Lord's Supper without a lawful excuse; to be ready to Contribute, according as God has prospered us, to the expenses of the Church and for the support of the ministry. These things we do Convenant and agree to hold sacred and to observe in the name of, and by the assistance of the holy Trinity.

RULES OF DECORUM

Art. 1st. All Conferences shall be opened and Closed with prayer.

Art. 2nd. The Pastor is ex officio Moderator of the Conference, and in case of his absence the Moderator shall be chosen by majority vote of the members present.

Art. 3rd. The Clerk shall be elected in like manner, and shall hold his office until he resigns his office, or is displaced.

Art. 4th. Conference shall be held on Saturday before the 4th Sunday in January, April, July and October. The names of the male members shall be Called and the absentees noted, and frequent absence from Conference shall be deemed a misdemeanor worthy of discipline.

Art. 5th. Only one person shall speak at a time who shall rise and address the Moderator; and the person speaking shall not be interrupted by any one but the Moderator. He shall strictly adhere to the subject under Consideration and in no wise reflect on a previous speaker.

Art. 6th. No person shall absent himself from the Conference without permission from the Moderator.

Art. 7th. No person shall speak more than three times on any subject without liberty granted by the Conference.

Art. 8th. No member during Conference, shall address another by any other title than that of brother.

Art. 9th. The Moderator shall not interrupt a member while speaking unless he violates a rule of decorum.

Art. 10th. The Moderator shall be allowed the privilege of speaking provided the Chair be filled.

Art. 11th. Any member who shall knowingly and willingly violate any of these rules, shall be reproved by the Conference as may be deemed proper.

Art. 12th. The proceedings of each Conference shall be read by the Clerk, before adjournment, Corrected if necessary and transscribed in the Church Book.

Art. 13th. Unanimity of sentiment shall be sought for in all matters, but if it Cannot be obtained, the question shall be decided by a majority of those present.

Art. 14th. The sisters shall have a voice in selection of Pastor, the reception of members into the Church, and their expulsion.

Church Officers

Pastors

George Matthias Thompson, 1842-1848
Martin Rudolph Forey, 1849-1851
Robert Henry Lanu, 1852-1855
Archibald McDowell, 1855-1873; 1875-1879
John Mitchell, 1873-1875; 1880-1882
Richard Tilman Vann, 1883
Charles Wesley Scarborough, 1884
Thomas Granberry Wood, 1885-1893
Samuel Saunders, 1894-1898
George Pinckney Harrill, 1898-1902
Albert Thomas Howell, 1903-1907; 1910-1912
Arthur Columbus Sherwood, 1908-1910
Quinton Clarence Davis, 1912-1913
William Harston Woodall, 1914
Thomas Calvin Keaton, 1915-1918
Julius Wesley Whitley, 1919-1925
William Richard Burrell, 1925-1932
Jesse Coleman Owen, 1933-1934
John Henry Bunn, 1935-1941
Paul Burton Nickens, 1941-1943
Junius Linwood Jones, 1943-1948
Warren Francis Taylor, 1948-1956
Rowland Shaw Pruette, 1956-1968
Thomas Herbert Caulkins, 1968 ——

Church Clerks

Lewis Thomas Spiers, 1848-1872; 1872-1878
Thomas D. Boone, 1872
Thomas Alexander Brett, 1878-1899
William G. Freeman, 1899-1904
W. B. Spencer, 1904-1906
Roger Watson, 1906-1907
John Catre Scarborough, 1907-1911
James D. Babb, 1911-1930
Herman H. Babb, 1930-1931
Susan Darden Sewell, 1931-1935
Ola A. Chitty, 1936-1950
Charles L. Revelle, Jr., 1950-1955
Bynum R. Brown, 1955-1970
Diane P. Dixon, 1970-1973
Herman Gatewood, 1973———

Church Treasurers

Jacob Parker, 1848- ?
George W. Spencer, 1882-1885
H. H. Cooke, 1885-1887
W. B. Spencer, 1887-1888
John W. Hoggard, 1888- ?
Thomas Alexander Brett, 1894-1899
William G. Freeman, 1899-1910
Uriah Watson, 1910-1912
James I. Griffin, 1912-1919
W. A. McGlohon, 1919-1925
James I. Crawford, 1925-1927

Herman H. Babb, 1927-1928
Ola A. Chitty, 1928-1930
Robert J. Britton, 1930-1932
E. W. Whitley, 1932-1947
Albert E. Hill, 1947-1956
R. A. Parker, 1956-1958
John P. Revelle, 1958-1962
James W. Hill, Jr., 1962-1964
Charles A. Chitty, 1964-1967
Stanley Dixon, 1967-1970
Jack A. Hassell, 1970 ———

Deacons

The date beside each name indicates the year service began as a deacon.

Benjamin Alexander Spiers, 1848
James H. Lassiter, 1848
Jethro R. Darden, 1864
L. D. L. Parker, 1873
G. D. Spiers, 1873
George W. Spencer, 1876
Emmett W. Nolley, 1876
H. H. Cooke, 1878
William G. Freeman, 1878
Thomas Alexander Brett, 1882
L. W. Bayley, 1882
Charles Wesley Scarborough, 1885
John Bruce Brewer, 1889
David A. Day, 1889
John Catre Scarborough, 1897
Uriah Watson, 1898
James D. Babb, 1910
John D. Barnacascel, 1910
C. E. Boyette, 1910
G. E. Lineberry, 1915
James I. Griffin, 1918
W. A. McGlohon, 1918
Douglas F. Payne, 1918
W. E. Jenkins, 1918
Walter P. Futrell, 1919
W. B. Edwards, 1926
J. A. Boyette, 1926
E. W. Whitley, 1926
C. J. Joyner, 1936
Joel Cooke Holland, 1940
C. W. Gardner, 1940
Harvey Copeland, 1940
George Gibbs, 1940
William Howell, 1948
Albert E. Hill, 1948
Millard E. Whitehead, 1948
*Harry W. Hill, 1948
*Robert V. Parker, 1948

*Horace Whitley, 1948
*Willie Williams, 1948
*J. M. Jenkins, 1948
*Charles Revelle, Jr., 1948
*Leonard Parker, 1948
*R. A. Parker, 1948
*Granville Howell, 1948
*Melvin Vinson, 1948
*James Hill, Jr., 1948
*Lawrence Parker, 1948
B. D. Bunn, 1949
Hiram C. Hill, 1958 ?
Wilson Johnson, 1960
Alton Parker, 1960 ?
L. E. Barnhill, 1961
Leo L. Bishop, 1961
John Prince, 1962
Ben C. Sutton, 1962
Maurice Burnette, 1962
Bynum R. Brown, 1962
Joe Dickerson, 1963
J. Craig Revelle, 1963 ?
Paul William Roden, 1963.
James G. Garrison, 1963
Charles L. Revelle, Sr., 1965 ?
Bob F. Hill, 1965 ?
J. Guy Revelle, Jr., 1968 ?
Carol Parker, 1968
Herman W. Gatewood, 1968
Jack A. Hassell, 1969
B. Franklin Lowe, 1970
Van Cuthrell, 1970
Richard Evans, 1971
Philip Royce, 1971
Clayton Lewis, 1971
Eley Whitehead, 1972
Steve Davenport, 1972
Joe Dixon, 1972
Percy Bunch, 1972

Those names marked * were elected to a "Junior Board of Deacons" in 1948. The Church has had two women elected to the position of deaconess: Mrs. T. B. Wynn (1930) and Mrs. E. B. Vaughan (1930).

Rosters of Church Members

The rosters which follow contain the names of (1) former members of the Murfreesboro Baptist Church and (2) current members of the church. All names have been gleaned from available records of admissons to membership found in the **Minutes** of Church Conference and/or other records of church membership which have been compiled.

The attempt has been made to include the names of all persons who have been members of the Murfreesboro Baptist Church since 1848. Omissions in the records will account for some omissions in the rosters. The attempt has also been made to avoid duplication of names. It is probable, however, that the names of certain women may appear twice: once under a maiden name at the time of admission to membership; once under a married name.

If there are errors or omissions which can be corrected by the reader, the church office would welcome information to this effect.

(1) Roster of Former Members, Murfreesboro Baptist Church

In this roster of former members an * indicates charter member of the church. Dates of admission and dismission and/or death are included when available. A name in **bold type** indicates a Negro member of the church.

A

Abbott, Keith (1958-1960)
Adams, Arelia (1961-1971)
Adkins, Jim Lee (1888-1905)
Adkins, Lavenia (1859-1887)
*Adkins, Sarah (1848- ?)
Adkins, Sarah R. (1871-1875)
*Adkins, Wade H. (1848- ?)
Allen, Josephine (?   )
Allen, Lonnie (1903- ?)
Allen, Loula Harris (1873-1886)
Alston, Mary Morris (1892-1895)
Amory, Ruth (1938-1942)
Anderson, Ella (1859-1863)
Anderson, Nora (1921- ?)
Andrews, Leah (? -1925)
Andrews, Peter C. (1901-1902)
Askew, Annie S. (1876-1882)
Askew, Elton W., Jr. (1938-1961)
Askew, Gilbert (? -1971)

Askew, Jewel (1920- ?)
Askew, Mollie Valentine (1871-1872)
Askew, Mary Louise (1906-1909)
Averette, Elvise (1948-1949)
Aydlett Naomi (1920-1921)

B

Babb, Annie Parker (1885-1945?)
Babb, Herman H. (1912-1952)
Babb, Herman H., Jr. (1938-1961)
Babb, James D. (1890-1930)
Babb, Morgan H. (1898-1930)
Babb, Jessie B. (1917-1945)
Bacon, Laura (1851- ?)
Bailey, Ann (1852-1858)
Bailey, Lucy (1866-1869)
Bailey, Rosa (1867-1869)
Baker, Charity (1857- ?)

87

Baker, Mattie E. (1882-1885)
Baker, Nannie (1877-1882)
Baker, Virginia Lee (1950-1965)
Baldwin, Myrtle (1915- ?)
Barber, Ellen (1894-1896)
Barber, Lettie (1894-1896)
Barber, W. A. (1894-1895)
Barkley, Evelyn Benthall (1938- ?)
Barnacascel, Annie (1885-1897: 1899-1919; 1920-1921)
Barnacascel, J. B. (1885-1897; 1899-1917)
Barnes, Jerry (1939- ?)
Barnes, Spencer (1968-1971)
Barnes, Mrs. Spencer (1968-1971)
Barrett, Betty Lou Hill (1944- ?)
Barry, Ora Thompson (1871-1878)
Bartley, Maggie (1910- ?)
Batchelor, Victor (1962- ?)
Battle, Fannie (1867-1868)
Battle, Jane Elizabeth (1860-1862)
Baugh, Mary (1851-1853)
Bayley, L. W. (1881-1882)
Bayley, Mrs. L. W. (1881-1882)
Beasley, Louise Ferebee (1910-1914)
Beasley, Joseph W. (1908-1946)
Beasley, Thelma Edwards (? -1938)
Beasley, Walter Clay (1910-1938; 1938-1944)
Beasley, William Freeman (1910-1914?)
Becker, Virginia Gardner (? -1939; 1940-1949
Beech, Cornelia (1897-1899)
Beecham, Lois (1959-1961)
Beekman, Adelia (1851- ?)
Belch, Fannie (1897-1899)
Bell, Corrine Forehand (1897-1904)
Bell, Margaret Thompson (1856-1872)
Bell, Vida (1939-1950)
Bennett, Rebecca Anne (1960-1965)
Bennett, Stephen Lowell (1972; 1973)
Bennett, Sybil Daughtry (? -1946
Benson, Alice Armistead (1857-1859)
Benthall, Beulah M. (1897- ?)
Benthall, Ovid (1897-1903)
Benthall, Pearla Watson (1904-1919)
Benyunes, Mark J. (1925?-1939)
Benyunes, Mrs. Mark J. (? -1945)
Bernard, Rosa (1884-1886)
Bidgood, Mary (? -1854)
Bishop, Ann (1956-1963; 1965-1966)
Bishop, L. L. (1956-1963; 1965-1966)
Bishop, Leanette (1966)
Bittle, Alice H. (1897- ?)
Bleck, Nannie (1881- ?)
Black, Ronald (1959-1960)
Blair, Charles (1941-1944)
Blanton, Abraham Lincoln (1949-1972)
Blowe, Mrs. C. E. (1969-1970)
Blowe, Raleigh H. (1941- ?)
Blowe, Raleigh, Jr. (1944- ?)
Blowe, Ophelia (1947-1950)
Blythe, Norman L. (1936-1938)
Bond, Mary (1867-1870)
Boone, Charles (1897-1900)
Boone, Grace Brown (1938-1947)

Boone, Lucy F. (1901- ?)
Boone, Julia (1897- ?)
Boone, Mollie Esther (1875-1878)
Boone, Thomas D. (1869-1872)
Boone, Mrs. Thomas D. (1869-1872)
Boone, W. E. (1943- ?)
Boone, Mrs. W. E. (1943- ?)
Bose, Janie Cree (1904-1908)
Boushall, Ann Thompson (1857-1866)
Boyette, C. E. (1895-1956)
Boyette, Brandel (? -1962)
Boyette, Charlie Archie (1906-1908)
Boyette, James A. (1886-1947)
Boyette, Katie Balance (1873-1897)
Boyette, Lucille (1897-1939)
Boyette, Mabel (? -1949)
Boyette, Mabel Jenkins (1913-1969)
Boyette, Nellie L. (1907-1939)
Boyette, Paul E. (1908-1925)
Boyette, Roy B. (1906-1911)
Boyette, Walter (1912-1913)
Boykins, Emma McClenny (1886-1887)
Bracey, Hobart (1940- ?)
Bracey, Patricia Walker (?   )
Branch, L. S. (?   )
Branch, Mrs. L. S. (?   )
Braswell, Marjorie Bridgers (1944- ?)
Brett, Edgar (1921-1933)
Brett, Mrs. Arthur (1950- ?)
Brett, Fanny (1953-1967)
Brett, James (1931- ?)
Brett, Lillian (1913)
Brett, Margaret (? -1938)
Brett, Mary Lee (1947- ?)
Brett, Paul (1913)
Brett, Sarah (1921-1951)
Brett, Thomas A. (1878-1899)
Brewer, Bruce (1886-1896)
Brewer, John B. (1882-1896; 1918-1920)
Brewer, Mrs. John B. (1882-1896; 1918-1920)
Brewer, Love Bell (1884-1887)
Brewer, Mamie (1892-1896)
Bridgers, Eston (1935-1942?
Bridgers, R. H. (1945-1973)
Bridgers, Sandra (1947- ?)
Briggs, Rosa Hines (1881-1889)
Brinkley, Kate Shields (1871-1874)
Brisson, James (1955-1959)
Brisson, Claire M. (1955-1959)
Britt, George (1949-1963)
Britt, W. F. (1897-1902; 1909)
Britton, Margaret S. (1852- ?)
Britton, Roy J. (? -1947)
Britton, Mrs. Roy J. (? -1947)
Brockwell, Mary Virginia (1901-1907)
Brooks, Joy Sandifer (1959-1967)
Brothers, Annie (1895-1897)
Brown, Amanda Baker (1866-1880)
Brown, Bettie F. (1886-1887)
Brown, Dorothy (1943-1944)
Brown, Elizabeth (1883-1897)
Brown, Ernest, Jr. (1952-1959)
Brown, Fannie (1894-1897)

Brown, Frank (1883-1897)
Brown, Grace (1882-1886)
Brown, Hattie (1894-1897)
Brown, Ida Majette (1871-1878)
Brown, Kathleen (1941-1948)
Brown, Harold (1958-1961)
Brown, Mrs. Harold (1958-1961)
Brown, King B. (1943-1944)
Brown, Mrs. King B. (1943-1944)
Brown, Laura (1943)
Brown, Margaret (1856- ?)
Brown, Minnie (1885-1897)
Bruner, Arthur C. (1910-1915)
Bruner, James D. (1909-115)
Bruner, Mrs. James D. (1909-1915)
Bruner, Willis James (1910-1915)
Bryant, Barbara Jean (? -1956)
Bryant, Carolyn Holland (? -1969)
Bryant, Catherine (1944- ?)
Bunch, Annie E. (1915- ?)
Bunch, Edith (1915- ?)
Bunch, Hazel (1904-1911?)
Bunch, John G. (1915- ?)
Bunch, Willie (1904-1911)
Bunn, Anna Frances (1949-1951)
Bunn, B. D. (1949-1951)
Bunn, Mrs. B. D. (1949-1951)
Bunn, Blonnie Dale (1949-1951)
Bunn, Elizabeth (1935?-1941)
Bunn, John H. (1935-1941)
Bunn, Mrs. John H. (1935-1941)
Bunn, John T. (1935?-1941)
Burchall, Eldridge (1921- ?)
Burke, Willard (? -1963)
Burke, Bernice Wilson (? -1963)
Burleson Frank (1964-1972)
Burleson, Helen (1964-1972)
Burleson, Lewis (1970-1972)
Burleson, Lynn (1970-1972)
Burnette, Sybil Daughtry (1940-1946)
Burrell, Beatrice (1925-1926; ? -1932)
Burrell, R. O. (1926-1932)
Burrell, Mrs. R. O. (1926-1932)
Burrell, W. R. (1926-1932)
Burrell, Mrs. W. R. (1925-1932)
Burroughs, Billy (1952-1967)
Butler, Claudie Powell (1874-1876)
Buxton, Bessie (1885-1890)
Bynum, Helen Brett (1921-1925; 1932-1942)
Bynum, Sally Freeman (1881-1886)
Byrd, Carolyn Kenney (1959-1964)
Byrd, Edward (? -1945)
Byrd, Gerald (1952-1973)
Byrd, Ivings (? -1952)
Byrd, Southgate (1947- ?)
Byrd, Mrs. Southgate (1947- ?)
Byrd, Wendell (1946- ?)
Byrum, Annie (1886)

C

Cadle, Betsy Ross (1955-1958)
Cadle, Lois (1955-1966)

Cadle, Ross A. (1955-1966)
Caddell, Brownie Trader (1894-1946)
Campbell, Ann (1944- ?)
Campbell, George, Jr. (1949- ? ; 1964-1966)
Campbell, Georgette Jeries (1964-1966)
Campbell, Mary E. (1951-1953)
Campbell, NeVa Futrell (1919-1965)
Carlyle, Nannie (1921- ?)
Carrick, J. L. (1937-1940)
Carrick, Mrs. J. L. (1937-1940)
Carroll, Bertha (? -1931)
Carter, Alpha Mae (1960-1962)
*Carter, Anastasia L. (1848- ?)
Carter, Carolina (1861- ?)
Carter, Mrs. C. H. (1926- ?)
Carter, E. E. (1914-1949?)
Carter, Mrs. E. E. (1945-1950)
Carter, Ellen V. (1861-1917)
Carter, Emma (1861-1864)
Carter, Joseph E. (1851-1858; 1859-1862)
Carter, Matthew F. (1873- ?)
Carter, Mollie L. (1874-1881)
*Carter, Priscilla (1848- ?)
Carter, Priscilla (1861-1862)
Carter, Theodore R. (1941-1953)
Cartwright, Barbara Byrd (1938- ?)
Caswell, Annie C. (1875- ?)
Catton, Loula Pitt (1871-1875)
Caudle, Leola (1955- ?)
Champion, Charles B. (1852-1854)
Champion, Mrs. Charles B. (1852-1854)
Chapman, Mary L. (1854- ?)
Cherry, Mary (1886-1892)
Chesson, Elouise (1884)
Chipman, Addie Watson (?   )
Chitty, Betty (1931-1941)
Chitty, Brenda (?   )
Chitty, Catherine (1939- ?)
Chitty, Charles A., Jr. (? -1966)
Chitty, Mrs. Charles A., Jr. (1965-1966)
Chitty, Doris (1941-1961)
Chitty, Evelyn Brett (1913-1917; 1921-1941?)
Chitty, H. L. (1936- ? ; 1944-1967)
Chitty, Mrs. H. L. (1936- ? ; 1944-1969)
Chitty, H. L., Jr. (? -1940; 1944-1964)
Chitty, Mrs. H. L. Jr. (1953-1964)
Chitty, H. W. (1915- ?)
Chitty, Florence Parker (1944-1958)
Chitty, Leon, III (1956-1964)
Chitty, Lois (1951- ?)
Chitty, Malcolm Reid (1944-1961)
Chitty, Margaret (1938-1942)
Chitty, Parthenia (1938-1945; 1949)
Chitty, Ola A. (1913-1967)
Chitty, Roderick R. (1943-1948)
Chitty, Mrs. Roderick R. (1943-1948)
Chitty, Redman (1929-1939)
Chitty, Thomas D. (1915-1953)
Chitty, Walter R. (1913-1917; 1921-1936)
Clark, Mrs. J. C. (? -1949)
Clark, Mildred Pipkin (1921-1949)
Clark, Ronnie (1958-1970)
Clark, Mrs. Ronnie (1964-1970)

Clark, Stanley (1966-1967)
Clayton, Mrs. Ocie (1919-1920)
Cleveland, Mrs. A. E. (1946-1964?)
Cleveland, A. E., III (1947-1964)
Cobb, Annie (1857-1865)
Cobb, Ruth (1875-1877)
Cohen, Mamie V. (1876-1880)
Coleman, Frances White (1953-1968)
Commander, Ida C. (1875-1886)
Cooke, Addie Mae (1952-1954)
Cooke, Alice (1926- ?)
Cooke, Annie (1890-1895)
Cooke, Effie (1903-1906)
Cooke, Eunice (1943-1950)
Cooke, H. H. (1878-1887)
Cooke, Mrs. H. H. (1878- ?)
Cooke, H. M. (? -1905)
Cooke, John Archie (1894-1909)
Cooke, L. M. (1940-1956)
Cooke, Mary (1886-1892)
Cooke, Mary Theresa (1894-1918)
Cooke, Nancy (1890- ?)
Cooke, Q. E. (1938-1972)
Cooke, William F., Jr. (1961-1963)
Cooper, Ann (1966-1969)
Cooper, Fred L. (1966-1969)
Cooper, Madge (? -1926)
Copeland, Mrs. L. E. (? -1906)
Copeland, Mary E. (1893-1898)
Copeland, Rorie (? -1941)
Copeland, Willie E. (1893-1898)
Copeland, Mrs. Willie E. (1893-1898)
Copeland, W. H. (? -1971)
Copeland, Mrs. W. H. (? -1965)
Cosby, Penny (1960-1961)
Cosby, Wayne (1960-1965)
Cosby, Mrs. Wayne (1960-1965)
Cotton, Juanita Hill (1938-1948)
Council, Martha (1854- ?)
Covington, Lula (1948-1949)
Cox, Annie (1857-1865)
Crawford, James I. (1926- ?)
Crawford, Mrs. James I. (1926- ?)
Creath, Louisa (1852-1855)
Cree, Beatrice (1903-1908)
Cree, Florence (1903-1908)
Croome, Laura Jane (1852-1853)
Croome, Martha A. (1852-1853)
Crouch, Warren G. (1966-1968)
Crowder, Shirley Bridgers (1942-1949)
Crumpler, Annie L. (1875-1880)
Cullen, Pauline Powell (1886-1890)
Cullen, Sadie (1910-1915)
Cullifer, Kathleen Chitty (1920-1932)
Curle, Reuben J. (1949-1950)
Cuthbertson, Phyllis Whitley (1952-1972)

D

Daile, Lou (? -1885)
Dale, Walter (1936- ?)
Daniels, Mamie (1968-1972)

Darden, Anna (1915)
Darden, Carrie (1915)
Darden, "Colonel" (1915)
Darden, Derusha (1938-1951)
Darden, J. B. (1892-1894)
Darden, Jethro (1858-1883)
Darden, J. H. (? -1950)
Darden, Joe W. (1915)
Darden, Mrs. J. H. (? -1951)
Darden, Mary Jane (? -1947)
Darden, Maggie (1915)
Darden, Mollie (1915)
Darden, Paul (1915)
Darden, Robert D. (1889-1891)
Darden, Rolf (1886-1889)
Darden, Sarah R. (1858-1890; 1895-1898)
Darden Sarah R. (1858-1890; 1895-1898)
Darden, W. R. (1894-1900)
Daughtry, Annie V. (1875-1889)
Daughtry, Helen Myrick (1855-1871)
Daughtry, Mrs. K. W. (1941-1962)
Davis, Belva (1905-1908)
Davis, Emma E. (1913)
Davis, Florence (1925- ?)
Davis, Mrs. L. E. (1882-1886)
Davis, Q. C. (1913)
Davis, Raleigh (1915- ?)
Davis, Rose Marie (1913)
Davis, Sarah E. (1913)
Davis, Thomas (1921- ?)
Davis, Z. L. (1919- ?)
Davis, Mrs. Z. L. (1919- ?)
Davis, Z. W. (1921- ?)
Day, Archie McDowell (1894-1901)
Day, Beatrice (1941- ?)
Day, David A. (1881-1903; 1913-1935)
Day, David A., Jr. (1913-1962)
Day, Ruth McDowell (1871-1937)
Day, William McDowell (1906- ?)
Dean, Dolores Odom (1944-1963)
Deanes, Clara (1915- ?)
Deanes, J. T. (1880-1883)
Deanes, William H. (1929-1944)
Deanes, Mrs. William H. (1938-1944)
Debnam, Mollie Warren (1876-1885)
Oelke, James A. (1867-1885)
DeLoatcne, Kenneth S. (1881-1910)
DeLoatche, Mrs. Kenneth S. (1881-1914)
DeLoatche, Mary Louise (1904-1914)
Denny, Lyndell (1926- ?)
Dilday, Connie (1956- ?)
Dobbs, C. C. (1921- ?)
Doughtie, Kelly (1940- ?)
Dozier, Virginia (1854- ?)
Downs, Mrs. Horace (1965- ?)
Drake, Mary Burgess (1944- ?)
Drake, Nina Moore (1867-1874)
Drake, Stanley T. (1939-1960)
Drake, W. F. (1858-1859)
Dudley, H. Haddon (1941-1944)
Dudley, Mrs. H. Haddon (1941-1944)
Duke, Donna (1962-1963)
Duke, Floye (1946-1963; 1966-1967)

Duke, Genevieve White (1946-1963)
Duke, James F. (1966-1967; 1968-1969)
Duke, Mrs. James F. (1966-1967; 1968-1969)
Duke Nora (1899-1903)
Duke, Ryland (?   )
Duke, Sylvia (1966-1967; 1968-1969)
Duncan, Ola Chitty (? -1944; 1946-1948)
Dunn, Alice Hope (1901- ?)
Dunning, Lizzie Tayloe (1876-1882)
Dunning, Mrs. William (1951-1964)

E

Early, C. R. (? -1960)
Early, Mrs. C. R. (? -1960)
Early, Mrs. Theo (1919-1921)
Edwards. Betty Grizzard (1960-1973)
Edwards, C. Stanley (1935-1942)
Edwards, Evelyn Whitley (1926-1942)
Edwards, Eunice (1884-1886)
Edwards, Lettie (1876- ?)
Edwards, W. B. (1924-1935)
Eldridge, Maria R. (1885-1886)
Eldridge, Mildred Alberta (1889-1899)
Eley, Clementine (1871-1872)
Eley, Ellen E. (1871-1872)
Elks, Charles (1958-1959)
Elks, Mrs. Charles (1958-1959)
Elliott, Beulah Hall (1903-1914)
Elliott, Carrie Moore (1875-1885)
Elliott, Odie (? -1933)
Ellis, Danny (?   )
Ellis, Linda (?   )
Ellis, Sue (1950- ?)
Emerson, Lillie (1893-1896)
Etters, Fred (1910-1920)
Etters, Mrs. Fred (1921 ?)
Eure, Wester (1940- ?)
Evans, Dorothy (1936-1939)
Evans, Louise Whitley (1947- ?)
Everett, Charles (1940-1942?
Everett, Elizabeth (1941-1942)
Everett, James B. (1892-1944)
Everett, Susan (1892-1922?)
Ewell, R. S. (? -1926)
Ezzell, J. M. (1922)
Ezzell, Mrs. J. M. (1922)

Fairless, Jessie Brandell (1931-1948)
Faison, Anna R. (1851-1852)
Faison, Judith Hill (1949-1968)
Faucette, Margarette (1914-1915)
Felts Elizabeth Watson (1915-1949)
Felts, Margianna Carter (1933-1951)
Fennell, Julia C. (1851-1853)
Fennell, Emmaline (1852-1853)
Ferebee, Annie E. (1867-1870

Fields, Nina (1871-1877)
Finch, Birdie (1874- ?)
Finch, Pattie Moore (1873-1881)
Fincher, Carolyn (1960-1961; 1961-1962)
Fincher, Sally Heath (1890-1910)
Fisher, Billy (1956-1962)
Fisher, Cathy (1956-1962)
Fisher, Norris (1943-1962)
Fisher, Pauline Anderson (? -1943; 1944-1962)
Fisher, Sallie (1917- ?)
Fitzhugh, India Ward (1885-1893)
Flack, Lula McClain (1914)
Flagg, Alice M. (1887-1889)
Fleetwood, Catherine (1938- ?)
Fleetwood, David (1952-1970
Fleetwood, Laura (1938- ?)
Fleetwood, Virginia Lee (1950- ?)
Fleetwood, Wilson (1938-1959)
Fleetwood, Mrs. Wilson (1938-1968
Fletcher, Alexena (? -1872)
Fletcher, Alvina (1857-1860)
Flythe, B. F. (1914-1948?)
Flythe, B. G. (1915- ?)
Flythe, Pauline (?   )
Forbes, Fannie (1947-1971)
Forbes, Jachin (1898-1906)
Forehand, Bettie M. (1876-1882)
Forehand, C. M. (1918-1967)
Forehand, John M. (? -1948)
Forehand, John M., Jr. (1963-1970)
Forehand, Lillian D. (1906- ?)
Forey, E. DeLancey (1854-1855)
Forey, M. R. (1851-1856)
Foster, Eugene B. (1960-1961)
Foushee, H. A. (1891-1893)
Freeman, Annie E. (1852-1855)
Freeman, George D. (1885-1887; 1897-1905)
Freeman, Harriett Adkins (1854-1871)
Freeman, Lucy Tyner (1877-1887; 1897-1906)
Freeman, William G. (1874-1887; 1897-1910)
Frizelle, William (1854-1874)
Fuller, Alese (1947-1950)
Futrell, Adelade (1875-1877)
Futrell, Alice (1921- ?)
Futrell, Bodie (?   )
Futrell, C. K. (1941-1942)
Futrell, Burton (1941-1942)
Futrell, Elton (1952- ?)
Futrell, Emma Jean (?   )
Futrell, Harold (1941-1942)
Futrell, Hortense (1941-1942)
Futrell, Joseph (1906- ?)
Futrell, Lokie M. (1918-1963)
Futrell, Marilyn (1956- ?)
Futrell, Nannie (1906-1939)
Futrell, Nedra Long (1948- ?)
Futrell, Myra B. (1938-1970)
Futrell, Patti Hill (1963- ?)
Futrell, Robert, Jr. (1950-1968)
Futrell, Rosa (1906-1928?)
Futrell, Royster (1941-1942)
Futrell, Mattie Johnson (1876-1888)
Futrell, Walter P. (1919-1967)

G

Galloway, Joan (?   )
Gardner, Chesley (? -1946)
Gardner, C. W. (1913-1958)
Gardner, Grace (1937-1941)
Gardner, Jennie Sewell (1904-1934)
Gardner, M. L. (1876-1890)
Gardner, William (1957-1959)
Garriss, Annie (1916-1918)
Garriss, R. R. (1916-1918)
Gary, Cora D. (1901-1904)
Gary, Fannie A. (1901-1943; 1950-1951)
Gary, Francis (1901- ?)
Gatling, Bettie Jean (?   )
Gatling, Claude (1901-1909)
Gatling, D. Bruce (1909-1915)
Gatling, Jefferson Davis (1896-1909)
Gatling, John (1906-1917)
Gatling, Louise (?   )
Gatling, Sarah D. (1857- ?)
Gatling, T. D. (1882-1885)
Gay, Carolyn (1936-1937)
Gay, Rosa Belle (1875-1880)
Gibbs, Ellie M. (1874-1877)
Gibbs, Gordon (1946-1948)
Gibson, Marvin (1965-1970)
Gibson, Mrs. Marvin, Sr. (1949- ?)
Gibson, Marvin, Jr. (? -1963)
Gibson, Sue Ellis (1950-1963)
Gill, John (1957-1962)
Gill, Sally (1957-1962)
Gilliam, Cornelia Valentine (1871- ?)
Gilliam, Cornelia Harrell (1857-1876)
Glover, Ann Brett (1947- ?)
Godwin, Lavenia (1903-1906)
Godwin, Rose (1912-1914; 1916- ?)
Graves, Mrs. C. C. (1926- ?)
Graves, C. D. (1894-1895)
Grant, Wilma (1920- ?)
Gravette, Ivey (1933-1937)
Gregory Eugenia (1939- ?)
Green, Elizabeth F. (1852- ?)
Green, Juliet Loving (1916-1917)
Greene, J. Craig (1970-1971)
Greene, Marti (1970-1971)
Greene, Minnie Brooks (1961-1963)
Greer, Josephine Anderson (?
Griffin, James I. (1920- ?)
Griffin, Sallie E. (1873-1882)
Griffith, Annie (1950- ?)
Griffith, Thelma (1921- ?)
Griffith, Ben (1920- ?
Griffith, L. W. (1906-1910; 1916- ?)
Griffith, Mrs. L. W. (1916- ?) ·
Griffith, Peter B. (1918- ?)
Griffith, Mrs. Peter B. (1918- ?)
Gravely, James (? -1965)
Gravely, Patsy Futrell (1947- ?)
Grizzard, Margaret (1950- ?)
Grizette, Eleneta (1873-1880)
Grogan, Robert (1953-1956)
Gwaltney, L. R. (1857- ?)
Gwaltney, Mrs. L. R. (1857- ?)

H

Harden, Mary Louise (1942-1946)
Hardison, Lois Chitty (1951-1960)
Hare, Ōzell Pipkin (1938-1968)
Hancock, Corrine Adkins (1875-1885)
Hargrove, Anna (1861)
Harker, Shirley (?   )
Harrell, Lloyd (1944-1965)
Harrell, Mollie W. (1876-1879)
Harrell, Oliver (1942-1973)
Harrell, Rex (1946-1950)
Harrill, George P. (1898-1902)
Harrill, Mrs. George P. (1898-1902)
Harrell, Sarah C. (1898-1901)
Harrington, Ella (1890)
Harris, Bessie (1879-1896)
Harris, Diane (1968-1969)
Harris, Donna (1966-1969)
Harris, George (1887-1891)
Harris, Harvey (1966-1969)
Harris, Joe Mac (1888-1892)
Harris, Julie Ann (1966-1969)
Harris, Roxie (1922- ?)
Harrison, Charles (1851-1853)
Harrup, Ruth Ellis (1947-1959)
Hart, Jane (1861)
Harvey, C. K. (1915- ?)
Harter, Ann Long (1965-1971)
Hatcher, Hardwick (1964)
Hatcher, Mrs. Hardwick (1964)
Hatcher, Katie (1964)
Heard, Brenda Chitty (? -1965)
Hedgepeth, Helen (1920- ?)
Hedgepeth, J. D. (1908-1911)
Hedgepeth, J. Wayland (1913- ?)
Hedgepeth, Laura Parker (1887- ?)
Hedgepeth, Mrs. M. E. (1897- ?)
Hedgepeth, Reuben (1913- ?)
Helms, Beadle (1934- ?)
Helms, Nan Puckett (1962 ?)
Henderson, Edith (1935- ?)
Hendricks, Henderson (1887-1889)
Henson, Poindexter S. (? -1855)
Hester, Joseph R. (1904-1906)
Hicks, Maurice (1876- ?)
Hill, Bernard (? -1952)
Hill, Cornelia (?   )
Hill, Ethel Boyette (1897-1966?)
Hill, Hiram C. (1948-1966)
Hill, James W., III (1955-1971)
Hill, Lydia (? -1854; 1861-1862)
Hill, Lydia H. (? -1854; 1861-1862)
Hill, Marie (1926- ?)
Hill, Martha (1959- ?)
Hill, Larry (1961-1962)
Hill, Mollie (? -1881)
Hill, Sarah Whitley (1937-1946)
Hill, Walter (? -1961)
Hill, Mrs. Walter (?-1961)
Hill, Juanita (1938-1948)
*Hines, Angeline Spiers (1848-1855 '
Hines, Bessie (1871-1881)
Hines, Burlie (1907-1911)

Hinnant, Frances Chitty (? -1941)
Hobbs, Rosa E. (1875-1877)
Hodgin, Arlene Tillery (? -1969)
Hoggard, John W. (1875-1877; 1878-1896)
Hoggard, William (1962-1963)
Holder, Rhodes (1932- ?)
Holland, Maggie (1873-1883)
Hollingsworth, Earnest (1941- ?)
Hollingsworth, William (1941-1950)
Holloman, E. Carter (1944-1950)
Holloman, Mrs. H. W. (1939-1941)
Holloman, S. D. (1899- ?)
Holloman, Samuel J. (1871-1936?)
Hooper, Ellen (1857-1860)
Hooper, Fanny (1859-1865?)
Hooper, Phillip (1857-1860)
Hooper, William (1859-1865?)
Hopkins, Conrad (1959-1961)
Horn, Gertrude (1915-1917)
Houghton, Jean (1959-1971)
Howard, Velva (1932-1934)
Howell, Albert Thomas (1903-1907)
Howell, Mrs. Albert Thomas (1903-1907)
Howell, Arthur R. (1901-1905)
Howell, Carrie Knight (1874-1888)
Howell, Charles M. (1908-1910)
Howell, Cyrus (1905-1908)
Howell, Dorothy Forehand (? -1948)
Howell, Flora (1899- ?)
Howell, Granville (1939-1948)
Howell, Jenny C. (1854)
Howell, Julia Frances (1908-1912)
Howell, Lorena (1898-1910)
Howell, Rosalind (1907-1910)
Huff, Myrtle (1930-1931)
Humbert, Ruth (1921)
Hyman, Annie (1881-1882)

I

Ingram, Annie M. (1904)
Ingram, Fannie (? -1906)

J

Jackson, Lizzie (1867-1871)
Jacobs, Mattie S. (1881-1886)
James, Fred (1963-1964)
James, Joanna (1963-1964)
James Robert Earl (1968-1972)
James, Mrs. Robert Earl (1968-1972)
James, Ruth Ann (1968-1972)
Jeanes, Opey Dew (1962-1967)
Jeanes, Virginia James (1961-1967)
Jenkins, Addie (1913- ?)
Jenkins, Annie (1913- ?)
Jenkins, Charles E. (1852-1853) .
Jenkins, Fannie (1919- ?)
Jenkins, Mrs. J. L. (?   )
Jenkins, Kate (1913-1917; 1918-1919; 1921- ? '

Jenkins, Lydia (1876-1878)
Jenkins, Rosa J. (1862- ?

Jenkins, Sallie Ann (1921-1970)
Jenkins, Stella (1885-1887)
Jenkins, Thomas (1887-1891)
Jenkins, W. E. (1913-1930)
Jernigan, Edna Porter (1931-1938)
Jester, Ella (1894-1895)
*Jiggetts, Margaret (1848-1861)
Johns, Paul E. (1901-1903)
Johnson, Ada (1937- ?)
Johnson, Carrie S. (1910-1916)
Johnson, Edith (1933- ?)
Johnson, Georgia Brown (1884- ?)
Johnson, J. T. (1955-1971)
Johnson, Linda Ann (1959-1966)
Johnson, Marilue (1960-1971)
Johnson, Marilyn (1955-1971)
Johnson, Mary Olivia (1959-1966)
Johnson, Milam (1955-1960)
Johnson, Mrs. Milam (1955-1960)
Johnson, Lynn (1955-1960)
Johnson, Norma (1956- ?)
Johnson, Wilson (1959-1966)
Johnson, Mrs. Wilson (1959-1966)
Johnson, Wilson, III (1961-1966)
Jones, Albert G. (1853-1854)
Jones, Annie B. (1878-1879)
Jones, Deleana (1943-1948)
Jones, Faye (1963-1967)
Jones, Harriett (1853-1854)
Jones, J. L. (1943-1948)
Jones, J. L., Jr. (1943-1948)
Jones, Mrs. J. L. (1943-1948)
Jones, James S. (1896-1898)
Jones, Linda (1965-1966)
Jones, Mollie (1896-1902)
Jones, Myra (1943-1948)
Jones, Virginia (1856- ?)
Jones, Virginia O. (1852-1853)
Jones, Winnie (1892- ?)
Jordan, Amanda Arthur (1858-1879)
Jordan, Susie Spurgeon (1906-1908)
Josey, Wortley Vaughan (? -1932)
Joyner, C. J. (1913-1915; 1936-1954)
Joyner, Mrs. C. J. (1936-1953?)
Joyner, Clara H. (1866-1877)
Joyner, D. C. (? -1926; ? -1937)
Joyner, Eliza M. (1871-1877)
Joyner, Eula B. (1873-1880)
Joyner, F. F. (1920- ?)
Joyner, Nida McCurry (1894-1912)
Joyner, T. (1939- ?)
Joyner, Vennie Hoggard (1886-1895)
Judkins, L. J. (1941-1943)
Judkins, Mrs. L. J. (1941-1943)
Judkins, L. J., Jr. (1941-1943)

K

Keaton, T. C. (1915-1918)
Keaton, Mrs. T. C. (1915-1918)
Keeler, Beatrice C. (1951-1966)
Key, Annie (1881-1886)
Kimbrell, Patricia (? -1961)

Kimbrell, Ralph (? -1961)
Kimprell, Mrs. Ralph (? -1961)
Kirk, Maggie Scarborough (1893-1896; 1900-1904)
Kitchin, Eva (1884-1886)
Knowles, Wayne (1961-1963)
Kornegay, Nancy Loftin (1857-1864)
Kornegay, Nettie Parrott (1871-1887)

L

Lacy, Sarah (1854)
Lambert, Ruth White (1939-1952)
Lancaster, Gail (1964-1970)
Lancaster, Mac (1964-1970)
Land, Louisa (1851-1853)
Land, Robert H. (1852-1855)
Land, Mrs. Robert H. (1852-1855)
Langston, Mrs. Morton (?)
Langston, Paulette Harmon (1968-1972)
Lanneau, Louise (1910-1912)
*Lassiter, Adaline A. (1848- ?)
Lassiter, Fannie (1876- ?)
Lassiter, Goldie (1925- ?)
*Lassiter, James H. (1848- ?)
Lassiter, Kate (1857- ?)
Lassiter, Kitty (1852- ?)
Lassiter, Robert (1860-1863)
Latham, Sarah (1851-1854)
Lawrence, Emily (?)
Lawrence, Eva Eldridge (1885-1897)
Lawrence, Mrs. F. W. (? -1913)
Layton, Melvin Quinton (1950-1952)
Layton, Mrs. Melvin Quinton (1951-1952)
Lee, Carolyn (1963-1971)
Lee, James (1963-1971)
Lee, James, Jr., (1963-1971)
Lee, Marjorie (1937-1957)
Lee, Robertd Welch (? -1962)
Lewis, James (1963-1970)
Lewis, Imogene (1963-1970)
Lewis, Nellie (1888-1896)
Lewter, Carlton (1945-1968)
Lewter, Mrs. Carlton (1964-1968)
Lewter, Fred A. (1874-1883; 1919)
Lewter, Joe C. (1949- ?)
Lewter, Ramond Burgess (1944- ?)
Liddell, DeAnna Forbes (1925-1926)
Lindsey, Edith (1926- ?)
Lineberry, G. E. (1914-1919)
Lineberry, Mrs. G. E. (1914-1918)
Lineberry, Margaret (1914-1918)
Lineberry, Ruth (1914-1918)
Liverman, A. D. (1940- ?)
Liverman, Mrs. A. D. (1945-1962)
Liverman, A. D., Jr. (1944- ?)
Liverman, Mrs. A. D., Jr. (1945-1966)
Liverman, Mrs. B. S. (1931-1933)
Liverman, C. E. (1898-1902)
Liverman, Felton (1913- ?)
Liverman, Frank (1952-1961)
Liverman, Martha (1911-1916)
Liverman, Viola (1875-1878)

Liverman, Walter (1949-1968)
Logan, L. H. (1920- ?)
Long, C. S. (1948-1951)
Long, Blanche Modlin (1948-1966)
Lowe, Maria (1859-1863)
Lowe, Mary A. E. (1918-1919)
Lowe, Mary S. (1901-1904)
Lowe, R. F. (1918-1919)
Lowe, R. W. (1918-1919)
Luke, Alice E. (1871-1880)
Lyon, Penelope (1861)

M

McAuley, Eddie (? -1968)
McAuley, Linda (1956- ?)
McBride, Marie (1961-1969)
McBride, Virgil L. (1961-1969)
McCabe, Mattie Brett (1897-1907)
*McCoy, Elizabeth Hatchell (1848-1864)
McCready, John D. (1957-1959)
McCready, Mrs. John D. (1957-1959)
McCready, Mary Winston (1957-1959)
McCullers, Mary M. (1913-1916)
McCulloch, Roy R. (1936-1937)
McCulloch, Mrs. Roy R. (1936-1937)
McCurry, Ernest (1894-1896)
McDade, Addie (1872- ?)
McDonald, Alice Payne (?-1948)
McDonald, William B. (1859-1960)
McDowell, Archibald (1856-1881)
McDowell, Archie (1874-1881)
McDowell, Eunice (1874-1881; 1882-1883;
                    1921-1946)
McDowell, Mary Owen (1856-1881; 1882-1905)
McFall, Joyce Bryant (1952-1968)
McGlauhon, W. P. (1899-1900)
McGlohon, Eunice Day (1906-1925; 1935-1969)
McGlohon, Rebecca (1940- ?)
McGlohon, W. A. (1913-1925; 1935-1950)
McGregor, Minnie (1932-1935)
McKnight, Edgar V. (1960-1963)
McKnight, Shirley (1960-1963)
McLenny, Lucy (1855- ?)
McMillan, Minnie (1876- ?)
Mackie, Mildred Britt (1954- ?)
Maddrey, James A. (1883-1889)
Maddrey, Laura J. (1873-1884)
Maile, Henrietta S. (1894-1897)
Majette, Beulah (1875-1880)
Major, Harriett (1960-1961)
Mangum, Helen Watson (1901-1916)
Mann, Eula Wise (1894-1910)
Mann, J. M. (1912- ?)
Manning, Bettie (1876-1880)
Martin, C. E. (? -1930)
Martin, C. H. (1876-1877)
Martin, Katherine Lois (1932-1934)
Martin, Mary L. (? 1931)
Martin, Russell (1942-1944)
Martin, Mrs. Russell (1942-1944)
Martin, Ruth Blowe (1943-1950)
Martin, Sarah Payne (1926-1941)

Martin, Virginia (? -1934)
Martin, Mrs. William F. (? -1957)
Masters, James (1958- ?)
Matthews, Carolyn (1960-1962)
Mattox, Pamela (1966-1970)
Mays, Bettie (1884-1886)
Merritt, Edith (1942- ?)
Merryman, Elizabeth J. (1861- ?)
Middleton, Helen (1933-1935)
Miller, William P. (1958-1960)
Miller, Mrs. William P. (1958-1960)
Mitchell, Hattie (1886-1887)
Mitchell, Henry Bingham (1906-1915)
Mitchell, J. D. (1947-1949)
Mitchell, Mrs. J. D. (1947-1949)
Mitchell, John (1874-1875; 1880-1883)
Mitchell, Maude (1905- ?)
Mitchell, Pauline (1867- ?)
Mitchell, Tina (1867-1870)
Mixon, F. O. (1951-1956)
Mixon, F. O., Jr. (1951- ?)
Mizelle, Margaret (? -1906)
Mizelle, Penny (1903- ?)
Mobray, Quessie Parker (1892- ?)
Modlin, Maywood (1932-1933)
Modlin, Madeline (1934- ?)
Moffatt, Annie (1867- ?)
Mooney, Hilda (1926- ?)
Moore, Anna H. (1871-1894)
Moore, Anne Ward (1851-1885)
Moore, Connie Dilday (1956-1972)
Moore, John Wheeler (1860-1885)
Moore, L. L. (1873-1885)
Moore, Louise (1884-1885)
Moore, Mollie (1882-1885)
Moore, Pattie Graves (1861-1877)
Moore, Percy (1959-1964)
Moore, Mrs. Percy (1959-1972)
Moore, R. T. (1875- ?)
Moore, W. G. (1905-1906)
Mooreland, Vernon (1961-1963)
Mooreland, Mrs. Vernon (1961-1963)
Morgan, H. (? -1915)
Morgan, Jordan E. (1904-1905)
Morgan, Karen H. (1936- ?)
Morris, Laura A. (1874-1880)
Morrisette, Lula B. (1871- ?)
Murfee, Lydia (1873-1877)
Munden, Clara Heddrick (1874-1892)
Murray, Jenny B. (1960-1962)
Musgrave, Hattie Pope (1881-1886)
Musha, Peggy Wiggins (1944-1965)
Myrick, Adona (1885)

N

Neal, Sallie McDonald (1871-1881)
Nelson, Charley (1913- ?)
Nelson, George L. (1949- ?)
Nelson, J. G. (1903-1950)
Nelson, Mrs. J. G. (1903-1929?)
Nelson, W. G. (1949- ?)
Nelson, Mrs. W. G. (1949- ?)

Nelson, Willie (1949- ?)
Nesbett, Margaret (1921- ?)
Newbern, Mamie (1934- ?)
Newbold, Jane (1860-1862)
Newcombe, Lillian (1885-1888)
Newsome, Carrie V. (1875-1883)
Newton, Ellen (1881-1882)
Newsome, Lizzie (1876-1878)
Newton, Lillian Gatling (1901-1909)
Nicholson, George E. (1958-1971)
Nicholson, Julia Scarborough (1899-1921)
Nicholson, Paula (?)
Nickens, Paul B. (1941-1945)
Nickens, Mrs. Paul B. (1941-1945)
Nipper, Beatrice (1951- ?)
Nolley, Emmett W. (1875-1882)
Nolley, Julia M. (1875-1882)
Nolley, Susan J. (1852-1883)
Norden, Susie (1921-1922)
Norfleet, Fannie Powell (1873-1882)
Norman, Irene Shannonhouse (1884-1889)
Nowell, Ada J. (1881-1882)

O

Oakley, Edith (1926- ?)
Oates, Fannie Nolley (1870-1886)
Oates, Mary E. (1851-1852)
Odom, Dolores (1944- ?)
Odom, Gene (1939-1972)
Odom, Jane (?)
Odom, Jesse (1931-1940)
Odom, J. W. (1920- ?)
Odom, John H. (1889-1891; 1892-1898)
Odom, Marion (1931- ?)
Odom, Paul (1929- ?)
Olive, Loula (1910-1912)
O'Neal, Rebecca Ann (1966-1967)
O'Neil, Annette Jordan (1966-1969)
Osborne, Walter (1962-1963)
Outland, Laura (1939-1942)
Outland, Norma Johnson (1956-1969)
Owen, J. C. (1933-1934)
Owen, Mrs. J. C. (1933-1934)
Owens, Sarah (1857)

P

Pace, Meter Parker (1875-1888)
Painter, Kate Sewell (? -1967)
Parker, Ada (1889-1890)
Parker, Ann (1856-1896)
Parker, Blannie (1918-1949)
Parker, Cellie (1920- ? ; 1935-1943)
Parker, Claude R. (1894-1899)
Parker, Mrs. D. L., Jr. (1947-1969)
Parker, D. L., III (1958-1971)
Parker, Edgar (1950-1963)
Parker, Shelby Davis (? -1963)
Parker, Elmer L. (1920- ? ; 1935-1960)
Parker, Mrs. Elmer L. (1944-1948)
Parker, Elton (?)
Parker, George W. (1938-1950)

*Parker, Goodman D. (1848-1887)
Parker, Gussie E. (1881-1883)
Parker, Henderson T. (1874-1880)
Parker, Herbert H. (1901-1903)
Parker, Mrs. Herbert H. (1892-1897)
*Parker, Jacob (1848- ?)
Parker, Jane Baldwin (1915- ?)
Parker, Jane Benthall (1918-1951)
Parker, John (1885-1899)
Parker, John W. (?)
Parker, Joan Hardin (1953-1958)
Parker, Joseph (1946- ?)
Parker, Mrs. Johnnie (1918-1957?)
Parker, L. D. L. (1870-1877)
Parker, Lawrence (1940- ?)
Parker, Lester (1947-1962)
Parker, Mrs. L. F. (? -1966)
Parker, Mary Eleanor (1860- ?)
Parker, Mabel (1892-1902)
Parker, Nancy (? -1926)
Parker, Paul (1967-1971)
Parker, Mrs. Paul (1967-1971)
Parker, Roy Boyette (1950-1966)
Parker, Mrs. J. Roy, Jr. (1939-1954?)
Parker, Robert V. (?)
Parker, Sadie (? -1895)
Parker, Sarah (1887-1895)
*Parker Sarah C. (1848- ?)
Parker, W. Gary (1918-1947)
Parker, Winifred (1926-1939)
Parrish, George (1961-1963)
Parrish, Katherine Payne (1931-1941)
Parrott, Ethel (1910-1915)
Patrick, Mary L. (1910-1911)
Patton, Millison Whitehead (1947-1962)
Paul Byron (1961-1966)
Paul, Mrs. Byron (1961-1963)
Payne, Dalton (?)
Payne, Douglas F. (1894-1909; 1912-1956)
Payne, Estelle B. (1915-1956)
Payne, Fred (1939- ?)
Payne, George D. (1881-1910; 1912- ?)
Payne, Mrs. George D. (? -1910)
Payne, Helen (1920- ?)
Payne, James Delke (1894-1909; 1915-1953)
Payne, Martha B. (1859-1860)
Payne, Paul A. (1893-1896)
Payne, Willie E. (1893-1896; 1908)
Pearce, Ann Deanes (1875-1897)
Pearce, Edward (? -1882)
Pearce, Ella (1907-1956)
Pearce, Lois (1951- ?)
Pearce, Marquerine Payne (1925-1946)
Pearce, Rebecca Parker (1940- ?)
Peebles, Nannie (1885-1886)
Pendergraph, Ella Mae (1919-1922)
Pendergraph, J. G. (1916-1922)
Pendergraph, John (1921-1922)
Perry, Julia Freeman (1875-1886)
Perry, Sadie T. (1892-1894)
Petteway, Ernest (1937-1944)
Peters, Annie Barnacascel (1904-1920)
Petty, Grace (1896)

Petty, W. O. (1896)
Petty, Mrs. W. O. (1896)
Perkins, Arizona (1853- ?)
Phelps, Ruth Harrell (1939-1952)
Phillips, Jane (1938-1947)
Phillips, Kay (1963-1966)
Phillips, Madeline (?)
Phillips, William (1963-1966)
Pierce, Chad (1967-1971)
Pierce, Mrs. Chad (1967-1971)
Piland, Emily (1938-1939)
Pipkin, Agnes (1902-1953)
Pipkin, Margie (1926- ?)
Pinner, Lydia (1937-1939)
Pledger, Leola G. (1929-1932)
Pledger, Margie (1929-1932)
Pledger, R. N. (1929-1932)
*Polkinhorn, Elizabeth (1848- ?)
*Polkinhorn, Samuel (1848- ?)
*Poole, Simon B. (1848-1851)
*Poole, William B. (1848-1871)
Pope, Janie (1945-1947)
Pope, Lallie M. (1881-1884)
Porter, Vera P. (1931-1950)
Powell, Lucy F. (1875- ?)
Powell, Martha A. (1875-1877)
Powell, Samuel B. (1874-1882)
Prather, Carol Beth (1960-1962)
Preston, Mary C. (1884-1889)
Prince, Ella (1881)
Prince, Jennie B. (1881)
Prince, John (1960-1965)
Prince, Kay Ulmer (1960-1965)
Pritchard, Eleanor (1852-1853)
Pritchard, Jane Brown (1944-1958)
Pritchard, Mary E. (1901-1903)
Pritchard, Phoebe (1852-1853)
Pritchard, William D. (1852-1853)
Pruden, Rassie (1955-1971)
Pulley, W. W. (1913- ?)

Q

Quarles, Julia Parker (1882-1886)

R

Ray, Jeanette (1854)
Ray, Mollie Harris (1871-1889)
Raynor, Fannie Jenkins (1913-1917; 1918)
Raynor, (1926- ?)
Raymond, Augusta (? -1926)
Rea, Charles (1861- ?)
*Rea, Joseph G. (1848- ?)
*Rea, Nancy (1848- ?)
Reed, Barbara (1955- ?)
Reese, Rosa (1852-1858)
Register, Carrie (1875)
Reiners, Willie (1930-1941)
Revelle, Floy Daniel (1937-1965)
Revelle, J. Craig (1953?-1963)
Rice, Helen S. (1901-1902)
Rich, Bessie (1884- ?)

Rich, S. M. (? -1886)
Richmond, Jesse (1926- ?)
Richmond, Margaret (1931-1934)
Ridgeway, Charles (1962-1964)
Ridgeway, Wilma (1962-1964)
Rittenhouse, Ruth (1925- ?)
Roan, Sarah Hall (1903-1913)
Robbins, Nora (1893-1896)
Robbins, Stella (1893-1896)
Rochelle, C. R. (1871-1878)
Roden, Bill (1962-1965)
Roden, Lila (1962-1965)
Roden, Paul (1962-1965)
Rodgers, Lelia Owen (1933-1934)
Rolfe, L. W. (1867-1879)
Rosser, Nancy (1939- ?)
Rowbotham, Tom (1949-1957)
Rowland, Rebecca (1852-1853)
Rumsey, Elizabeth (1921- ?)
Russell, Nancy (1856-1857)

S

Salisbury, Sallie (1892)
Sample, James (1963)
Sanders, Gordon (1936-1937)
Sanderson, Evelyn Davenport (? -1940)
Sandifer, Billy Joe (1964-1966)
Sandifer, Charley L. (1959-1966)
Sandifer, Jean (1959-1966)
Sandifer, Joy Y. (1959-1966)
Sandifer, Lonnie (1959-1966)
Sasser, Lonnie (1962-1972)
Sasser, Mrs. Lonnie (1962-1972)
Satchwell, Martha (1851- ?)
Saunders, Adelaide (1894-1898)
Saunders, Samuel (1894-1898)
Saunders, Samuel, Jr. (1894-1898)
Scarborough, Anna Eldridge (1885-1916)
Scarborough, Annie R. (1899- ?)
Scarborough, Hartwell V. (1897-1900; 1902-1909)
Scarborough, Helen (1890-1896)
Scarborough, Charles Wesley (1883-1909; 1912-1918)
Scarborough, (1883-1885)
Scarborough, John C. (1897-1911; 1916-1917)
Scarborough, Mrs. John C. (1897-1911; 1916-1917)
Scarborough, Maggie Saltzman (1885-1896)
Scarborough, Paul (1893-1896)
Schaible, Valerie (1929-1936)
Schurr, Charles (1957-1959)
Schurr, Mrs. Charles (1957-1959)
Scott, Clair (1969-1971)
Scott, James (1969-1971)
Scott, Julia (1885-1915)
Scott, N. Bascom (1931-1941)
Sears, William H. (1875-1885)
Sebrell, Kate Whitehead (1873-1888)
Sessoms, J. D., Jr. (1913- ?)
Sewell, C. B. (1920)
Sewell, Charley McLane (1894-1933)
Sewell, Clyde M. (1901-1907)
Sewell, Floyd W. (1894-1907)
Sewell, J. D. (1926-1949)

Sewell, Jessie (1926-1949)
Sewell, Mrs. J. M. (? -1947)
Sewell, John Mitchell, Jr. (1944-1960)
Sewell, Martha D. (1883- ?)
Sewell, Paul D. (1920-1971)
Sewell, Rensselaer "Rentz" (1885;
                              1901- ?)
Sewell, Mrs. R. L. (1892- ?)
Sewell, Robert G. (1920-1973)
Sewell, Susan Darden (1920-1972)
Sewell, Vernon (1913- ?)
Shannonhouse, Donna (1881)
Sharp, Gladys (1905-1909)
Sharp, Lalie (? -1880)
Shaw, Emma D. (1876-1880)
Shaw, Harriett P. (1851-1852)
Shaw, William A. (1851-1852)
Shell, Shirley (1947-1951)
Sheppard, Lyman (?   )
Shields, Pattie F. (1874-1876)
Shortridge, Ellen B. (1874-1884)
Simmons, Hortense (1963-1966)
Simmons, Viola G. (? -1878)
Slate, Lib (1956-1959)
Slate, T. A. (1956-1959)
Slate, Mrs. T. A. (1956-1959)
Slate, Tommy (1956-1959)
Sledd, Gladys (1939-1941)
Smallwood, Jimmie Graves(1871-1878)
Smith, Emma E. (1893-1896)
Smith, Fanny A. (1854)
Smith, Francis (1893-1896)
Smith, Joy (1955-1968)
Smith, Joe D. (1960-1967)
Smith, Judith (1857-1864)
Smith, Julia (1857- ?)
Smith, Lola (? -1926)
Smith, Louise Gatling (? -1963)
Smith, Mary (1933- ?)
Smith, Pamela (1852- ?)
Smith, Susan (1859-1892)
Sodeman, Lowell F. (1936-1937)
Souter, Beryl (1921-1926)
Spaulding, Clyde (1943- ?)
Spaulding, J. H. (1943-1947)
Spaulding, Mrs. J. H. (1943- ?)
Spaulding, Margaret (1943)
Spencer, Charles H. (1872- ?)
Spencer, Emma (1875-1898; 1904-1907)
Spencer, Emma (1892- ?)
Spencer, George W. (1872-1894)
Spencer, Job S. (1890-1893)
Spencer, Mary Jane (1874- ?)
Spencer, Melissa (1872-1894)
Spencer, W. B. (1875-1898; 1904-1907)
*Spiers, Benjamin A. (1848-1873)
Spiers, B. S. (? -1877)
Spiers, Elizabeth (1851- ?)
Spiers, Francis T. (1851- ?)
Spiers, Genie (1867- ?)
Spiers, Helena (1864-1872)
Spiers, J. C. (1874-1878; 1879-1884;
                              1910- ?)

Spiers, L. H. (1875-1878)
*Spiers, Lewis T. (1848-1879)
*Spiers, LaVenia C. (1848- ?)
*Spiers, Mary A. (1848- ?)
Spiers, Nannie (1884-1885)
Spiers, Stowe (1867- ?)
*Spiers, Thomas (1848- ?)
Spiers, W. M. B. (1875-1882)
Spring, John (1963-1969)
Spring, Mrs. John (1963-1969)
Spring, Liz Ann (1966-1969)
Spruill, Clara (1892)
Spruill, Margaret (1950-1969)
Spruill, May (1892)
Spruill, N. M. P. (1875 ?)
Stephens, Bertha Vaughan (1949-1951)
Stephens, Paul (1949-1951)
Stephenson, A. C. (1880-1884)
Stephenson, Bernice Day (? -1966)
Stephenson, Bobby (1939- ?)
Stephenson, Claud M. (1913-1916)
Stephenson, Elizabeth W. (1875-1876)
Stephenson, Fannie M. (? -1891)
Stephenson, Mrs. Lee (1941-1949)
Stephenson, Nannie (1882- ?)
Stephenson, Sue (1962-1963)
Stewart, Jack (1961-1965)
Stewart, Mrs. Jack (1961-1965)
Stewart, Sheila (1962-1965)
Stewart, Susan (1962-1965)
Stillman, Christine (? -1937)
Stokes, Lewis T. (1956- ?)
Storey, Charles Rufus (? -1960?)
Storey, Mrs. Charles R. (? -1958?)
Storey, Mrs. D. F. (? -1959)
Storey, Frank W. (1887- ?)
Stradley, Mrs. W. C. (? -1945)
Stuart, Evelyn Bell (1939-1941)
Sumner, Ellen J. (1897-1901; 1906-1933)
Sumner, Mrs. J. W. (1930?- ?)
Sumner, L. F. (1897-1901; 1906- ?)
Sumner, Walter (1953-1970)
Sutton, L. H., III (1962-1963)
Sutton, Karen (1962-1963)
Swain, James J. (1968-1971)
Swain, Mrs. James J. (1968-1971)
Sykes, Eleanor (1867-1868)

T

Tate, Cissa Spencer (1879-1886)
Tayloe, Bessie T. (1885-1887)
Tayloe, Carrie W. (1871-1874)
Tayloe, Fannie Harrell (1881-1885)
Tayloe, Lillie (1876-1881)
Taylor, Ann R. (1866-1868)
Taylor, Cora H. (1951-1952)
Taylor, Frances (1948-1956)
Taylor, Julia W. (1857-1867)
Taylor, Margaret (1921- ?)
Taylor, Nettie (1903-1906)
Taylor, Mrs. J. P. (1947-1958)
Taylor, Warren F. (1948-1956)

Taylor, Warren F., Jr. (1948?-1956)
Taylor, W. M. C. (1903-1906)
Terry, Mrs. M. C. (1926- ?)
Thigpen, Estelle (1957-1961)
Thatch, Addie (1857-1859)
Thomas, Louise Sewell (? -1947)
Thomas, Grace (? -1926)
Thomasson, Julia Brewer (1885-1896; 1918-1920)
Thompson, Ann (1965-1968)
Thompson, Ann Rodes (1965-1968)
Thompson, Mary B. (1872-1873)
Thompson, M. B. (1872-1875)
Thompson, Paul (1965-1968)
Thompson, Vander (? -1967)
Thompson, Sarah E. (1871-1873)
Tillery, Arlene (?   )
Tillery, Faye (1956- ?)
Timberlake, Clellie (1892-1896)
Timmons, Elaine (1947-1960)
Trader, Dodge (1940- ?)
Trader, Sarah R. (1881-1890)
Traylor, Mrs. Buxton (? -1938)
Trentham, Nannie (1874- ?)
Triplett, Paula Kathryn (1959-1960)
Tucker, Genevieve (1937-1945)
Tucker, Rebecca McGlohon (1941-1967)
Tudor, Kathy (1966)
Turner, Lettia (1877-1879)
Turnley, Annie (1921- ?)
Turnley, Elizabeth (1921- ?)

U

Underwood, Fannie Boyette (1897-1906; 1917-1968)
Urquhart, Maggie (1884- ?)
Upton, Addie (1886-1894)

V

Vail, Sue (1871-1872)
Vann, Abbie (? -1904)
Vann, Annie Belle (1910- ?)
Vann, Annie Griffith (1950-1960)
Vann, Betty (1969- ?)
Vann, Elmer (1950-1960?)
Vann, Geulia (1897-1899)
Vann, Mrs. Jarvis (1951- ?)
Vann, Josephine H. (1897-1899)
Vann, Katherine (1969- ?)
Vann, Linda Ellis (? -1963)
Vann, Lois (1950- ?)
Vann, Mary H. (1910-1913)
Vann, Nannie C. (1875-1877)
Vann, Preston S. (1898-1902; 1920-1923)
Vann, Mrs. Preston H. (1898-1902; 1920-1923)
Vann, Richard Tilman (1882-1884)
Vaughan, Erastus B. (1920-1924)
Vaughan, Lucy (1924-1943)
Vaughan, Nancy Parker (1920- ?)
Vaughan, Wayne (? -1961)
Vernon, Frances (1930- ?)
Vick, Winifred Parker (? -1969)
Vick, Lizzie (?   )
Vinson, Emma Jean Futrell (?   )
Vinson, Elizabeth Crump (? -1884)
Vinson, Mrs. J. C. (1885- ?)

Vinson, Linwood (1910-1912)
Vinson, Robert (1950-1965)
Vinson, Mrs. Robert (1944-1965)

W

Wade, Maggie (1926- ?)
Wade, Ralph (1910-1915)
Walker, Barbara Jane (1958?- ?)
Walker, Mary Ray (1913-1918)
Walker, Patricia (1958- ?)
Walker, Mrs. R. S. (1951- ?)
*Wall, Carter H. (1848-1850)
Wall, L. W. (1911-1914)
Wallace, Dorothy A. (1968-1973)
Wallace, L. M. (1958-1973)
Walters, Mark K. (1884-1885)
Walters, Mary A. (1852- ?)
Ward, John (1951- ?)
Ward, Mrs. John (1951- ?)
Ward, Mildred Watson (1921-1940)
Warren, George (1921- ?)
Warren, T. K., Sr. (1937- ?)
Warren, Mrs. T. K., Sr. (1937-1961)
Warren, W. Jesse (1920-1937)
Warren, Mrs. W. Jesse (1920-1942?)
Warrick, Jean Elizabeth (?)
Warrick, Rives (? -1953)
Wasden, Dora (1901- ?)
Waters, Cecil (1914- ?)
Waters, Donald (1914-1919)
Waters, Edward W. (1914-1922)
Waters, Mary (1915-1922)
Waters, Mary Allen (1914-1916)
Waters, Walter (1915- ?)
Watson, Burchair (1912- ?)
Watson, Ellen E. (1871-1872)
· Watson, Jessie (1910-1915; 1920- ?)
Watson, Mary Jane (1871-1872)
Watson, Pattie (1898-1946)
Watson, Richard Bland (1908-1915; 1920-1941)
Watson, Roger (1899-1918)
Watson, Mrs. Roger (1914-1918)
Watson, Uriah (1898-1918)
Weaver, Charles P. (1923-1926)
Weaver, Mrs. Charles P. (1923-1926)
Weaver, Sally (1871- ?)
Webb, Emma (1881-1890)
Welch, H. H. (1953-1971)
Welch, Mrs. H. H. (1953-1971)
Weston, Margianna (1859-1863)
Wheeler, Catherine F. (1851-1866)
Wheeler, Virgil (1851- ?)
Whilding, Susan G. (1877- ?)
Whitaker, Barry Eugene (1963-1971)
White, Bettie S. (? -1880)
White, Mrs. B. F. (1892- ?)
White, Elizabeth (?)
White, Georgia Spencer (1879-1893)
White, Joseph H. (1895-1900)
White, Hugh (1920-1965)
White, Huyler (1893-1952)
White, Kathryn Bryant (1944-1960)

White, Laura Outland (. ?)
White, Lillian Hoggard (1923-1933)
White, Naomi Warren (1920- ?)
White, Patty W. (1862-1869)
White, Phillip (1897-1901)
White, Robert B. (1884-1893)
White, Sally (1945-1950)
White, Sally C. (1873-1896)
White, Mrs. S. C. (1896- ?)
White, Sarah J. (1873-1880)
Whitehead, M. E. (1937-1963)
Whitehurst, Josie (1890- ?)
Whitfield, Nina (1871- ?)
Whitley, Annie (? -1964)
Whitley, Barbara (1945- ?)
Whitley, Charles (1945-1960)
Whitley, Clarence (1938- ?)
Whitley, Crystal Liverman (1951-1966)
Whitley, Elaine (1947- ?)
Whitley, Eunice R. (1933- ?)
Whitley, E. W. (1926-1956?)
Whitley, Mrs. E. W. (? -1950)
Whitley, Horace (1937-1949)
Whitley, Mrs. Horace (1946-1949)
Whitley, John L. (1947-1960)
Whitley, Joseph B. (?)
Whitley, Mrs. Joseph B. (1954-1959)
Whitley, Julius W. (1919-1925)
Whitley, Mrs. Julius W. (1919-1925)
Whitley, Landis (1937- ?)
Whitley, Mary (1918- ?)
Whitley, Mary E. (1941-1952?)
Whitley, Mary Wise (1897-1912)
Whitley, Maxine (1921- ?)
Whitley, Nancy (1958- ?)
Whitley, Ryland (1921-1966)
Whitley, Shirley Mae (1944- ?)
Whitley, Stanley (1950-1969)
Whitley, Mrs. Stanley (1950-1969)
Whitley, Mrs. Tom (? -1971)
Whitley, Winnie (1920)
Whittingill, Eleanor (1933- ?)
Wigginsn C. H. (1946-1955?)
Wiggins, Isaac Andrew (1904-1954)
Wiggins, Jean (?)
Wiggins, Mary E. (1904-1936)
Wiggins, Naomi T. (1904-1958)
Wiggins, Peggy (1944- ?)
Wiggins, Sallie (1904- ?)
Wiggins, Tommie (1947-1960)
Wiley, Doris (1926- ?)
Wiley, Mary M. (? -1911)
Wilkins, Mary Etta (1875-1876)
Williams, Bill (1958-1959)
Williams, Mrs. Bill (1958-1959)
Williams, Billy (1958-1959)
Williams, Billy J. (1962-1965)
Williams, Mrs. Billy J. (1962-1965)
Williams, Clara Forehand (?)
Williams, C. V., Jr. (1950-1951)
Williams, Mrs. C. V., Jr. (1950-1951)
Williams, Eleanor Payne (1926-1949)
Williams, Fred (1950- ?)

Williams, Mrs. Ernest (? -1949)
Williams, Jimmy (1958-1959)
Williams, Lillian (1916-1917)
Williams, Orelia (1875-1876)
Williams, S. E. (1852-1853)
Williamson, Frank (1888-1895)
Williamson, Joe C. (1885-1914)
Williamson, Sylla (1886- ? ; 1914-1919)
Williford, Meddie Burden (1882-1886)
Williford, Lou (? -1931)
Willis, Vesta (1929- ?)
Willoughby, Inez (1932- ?)
Willoughby, Mary Vinson (1944- ?)
Wilson, Jane Brown (1931-1932)
Wilson, Lou (1871-1874)
Wilson, Lula Covington (1948-1949)
Wilson, Mary Allie (1867-1869)
Wilson, Mona (1912-1914)
Winborne, Ella M. (1875-1883)
Wimbish, Cadyle (1967-1969)
Wimbish, Jo (1967-1969)
Winston, Elizabeth White (1949-1968)
Wise, Bucky (1960-1965)
Wise, Emma Spencer (1903-1916)
Wise, Gloria Jean (? -1960)
Wise, Kenneth R. (1874-1892; 1901- ?)
Womble, Louise (? -1943)

Wood, Donald S. (1956-1958)
Wood, Mrs. Donald S. (1956-1958)
Wood, Dora Askew (1889-1894)
Wood, Jenny (1861-1862)
Wood, Laura (1874-1877)
Wood, Mary (1886-1894)
Wood, Sophia (1886-1894)
Wood, Thomas G. (1889-1894)
Woodall, W. H. (1914)
Woodall, Mrs. W. H. (1914)
Woodard, Emma J. (1874-1875)
Woodcock, Jennie (1903-1911)
Woodland, Robert (1951- ?)
Woodward, Bettie (1876-1881)
Worrell, Betsy Wiggins (1942-1964)
Worrell, George (1861-1864; 1865- ?)
Worsley, Ida V. (1876)
Worthington, Julia Wheeler (1857-1866)
Wright, Gladys Byrd (1920-1949)
Wright, Lillian (1884-1886)
Wynn, Essie (1911-1917)

Y

Young, William C. (1959-1960)
Young, Mrs. William C. (1959-1960)

(2) Current Members, Murfreesboro Baptist Church.

The following roster includes the names of all current members of Murfreesboro Baptist Church as of May 22, 1973. The membership is grouped by families. The date following each name indicates the year in which each person became a member of the church. An * indicates non-resident members, as per the official church roll.

A

Allen, Walter (1965)
  Allen, Myrna (1965)
  Allen, Donnie (1967)
  Allen, Michael (1965)
*Allsbrook, Linda McAuley (1956)
*Anderson, Mrs. J. M. (1929)
*Anderson, Jimmy (1947)
  Askew, Elton W. (1931)
  Askew, Gladys (1931)
  Askew,   James   M.   (?)
  Askew, Mrs. James M. (?)
*.Askew, L. C. (1938)

B

*Baggett, Mrs. Fred (?)
  Baker, Ethel (1957)
*Ballance, Jane Hill (1956)
  Banks, E. P. (1943)
    Banks, Eunice (1940)
  Banks, E. P., Jr. (1946)
  Banks, Billy Week (1952)
*Barkley, Cynthia Hill (1959)

*Barnes, Mary (1967)
*Barnes, Jackie Liverman (1958)
*Barnhill, L. E. (1960
  *Barnhill, Eddie (1965)
  *Barnhill, Kim (1968)
  *Barnhill, Toni (1968)
  Barrett, Earl (1968)
    Barrett, Louise (1968)
  Batchelor, Betty (1962)
    Batchelor, David (1972)
    Batchelor, Jonathan (1968)
    Batchelor, Paul (1968)
*Beamon, Annis (1958)
  Beatty, Shirley (?)
    Beatty, Chris (1966)
  Belch, Lela (1947)
  Belch, Waverly (1944)
*Benjamin, Jo Ann Smith (1947)
  Bennett, Steve (1972)
*Benthall, J. E. (?)
  *Benthall, Mrs. J. E. (?)
  Benthall, Mrs. Tommy (?)
*Bess, Earl (1943)
  Bess, Russell, (?)

Bess, Shelby (?)
Bess, Kay (1967)
Bess, Sally (1943)
Bird, Marion (1970)
    Bird, Virginia (1970)
    Bird, Tommy (1970)
Blanton, Beverly Jordan (1959)
Blanton, Linda V. (1968)
Blowe, Nannie (1941)
*Bolivia, Barbara Reed (1955)
*Bowden, Betty Jean (?)
*Boykin, Robbie Lee (1947)
Brett, Jennie Sue (1939)
Brett, Kathy Copeland (1967)
Bridgers, Mrs. R. H. (1945)
Bridgers, Ronald (1955)
*Bridgers, Wayne K. (1960)
Britt, Dorothy (1944)
Britt, Southgate (1947)
Britt, W. F. (1938)
    Britt, Louise (1938)
    Britt, Louise Jenks (1960)
Britt, Walter B. (1950)
    Britt, Rousseau (1950)
    Britt, Jennie (1969)
Britt, William (1957)
    Britt, Clara (1957)
Britt, J. W., Jr. (1958)
*Britt, Wilson, Jr. (1959)
Brown, Bynum R. (?)
    Brown, Gracie (1972)
*Brown, Charles O. W. (1964)
*Brown, Mrs. Ernest (1952)
*Brown, Mrs. Garland (1964)
Brown, Grace Pearce (1918)
*Brown, Mary Lee Hill (1956)
*Bryant, Billy (1947)
Bryant, Richard (1939)
    Bryant, Jessie (?)
    Bryant, Steve (1963)
Bryant, W. C., Jr. (?)
    Bryant, Paul (1967)
Bunch, Percy (1966)
    Bunch, Lynette (1966)
    Bunch, Fran (1968)
    Bunch, Julie (1970)
    Bunch, Mrs. N. W. (1966)
*Burden, Cynthia (1966)
*Burden, Michelle (1964)
*Burgess, Joe (1947)
*Burgess, Rita Whitley (1959)
Burnett, Don (1965)
    Burrnett, Linda (1965)
Burnette, Maurice E. (1958)
    Burnette, Butch (1958)
    Burnette, Craig (1966)
    Burnette, Steve (1966)
*Byrd, Benny (1961)
*Byrd, Charles (1961)
*Byrd, Donnie (1961)
*Byrd, Frances (1942)
Byrd, Gene (1961)
Byrd, Tommy (1958)

Byrd, Nell (1958)
*Byrd, Mrs. W. L. (1942)

C

*Carson, Morris (1966)
*Carson, Betty (1966)
*Carter, Alpha Mae (1960)
*Cason, Rachel Forbes (1952)
*Casey, Allen Jay (1960)
Caulkins, Thomas H. (1968)
    Caulkins, Ann (1968)
    Caulkins, Charlene (1968)
    Caulkins, Bonnie (1968)
Chamblee, James M. (1960)
Chamblee, Karen (1973)
Chitty, Charles A. (1937)
    Chitty, Elizabeth (1941)
Chitty, Jerry N. (?)
Chitty, Janice (?)
    Chitty, Thomas (1956)
Chitty, Eva Boyette (1905)
Clark, Herman (1971)
    Clark, Judy (1971)
Clark, Jerry (?)
    Clark, Norma (?)
Clark, Walter (1939)
    Clark, Marie (1939)
Collins, Clifton S. (1964)
    Collins, Janet (1964)
*Compton, Donna Britt (1960)
Cooke, Bruce (1958)
    Cooke, Elaine (1958)
Cooke, James (?)
Cooke, Louise (1938)
*Cooke, Q. E., Jr. (1949)
*Cooper, Frederick L., III (1966)
*Cooper, Thomas (1966)
Copeland, George (1931)
    Copeland, Louise (1950)
Cox, Douglas (1971)
    Cox, Amanda (1971)
Cox, Lynn (1971)
Cox, Susan (1971)
Crouch, Anna Belle (1958)
Cuthrell, Van (1968)
    Cuthrell, Linda (1968)
    Cuthrell, Peggy (1968)

D

Dacus, Edwin (1970)
    Dacus, Martha (1970)
Davenport, Steven (1963)
    Davenport, Pat (1963)
    Davenport, Liz (1963)
    Davenport, Joy (1963)
*Davenport, Steven, Jr. (1963)
*Davenport, Kathy Jenkins (1960)
*Davis, Carroll (1964)
    *Davis, Mrs. Carroll (1964)
*Davis, Martha Holland (1956)
*Day, David Day, III (1947)
*Day, Mary Mallory (1939)
    Day, Janet Benthall (?)

*Deanes, Sidney (1938)
*Deanes, Mrs. Sidney (1938 ?)
Deanes, Mrs. W. E. (1920)
Dickerson, Joe (1957)
  Dickerson, Esseyl (1957)
  Dickerson, Debbie (1966)
*Dickinson, Calvin (1961)
*Dickinson, Charlene (1961)
Dilday, Earl (1971)
  Dilday, Joy (1971)
Dilday, Howard (1967)
  Dilday, Mabel (1967)
*Dilday, Mary Alice (1963)
Dilday, Raymond (1944)
  Dilday, Ruth (1944)
Dixon, Joseph E. (1963)
  Dixon, Diane P. (1947)
, Dixon, Stanley (1953)
  Dixon, Clyde Merrell (1953)
  Dixon, Stan (1966)
  Dixon, Cynthia (1970)
Doughtie, Dodson (1946)
  Doughtie, Lacy K. (1946 ?)
*Doughtie, Martha (1959)
Duke, Ola (1937)
  Duke, Shell (1939)
Duke, Willie (1961)
  Duke, Betty (1961)
  Duke, Tula (1966)

E
*Edwards, Betty Ruth (?)
*Edwards, Patti Shewbart (?)
*Edwards, Waverly (?)
Edwards, W. W., Jr. (1965)
  Edwards, Patricia B. (1962)
*Ellis, H. B. (?)
*Ellis, Mrs. H. C. (1949)
*Ellis, William (1947)
Emery, Ann (1970)
  Emery, Joseph (1970)
  Emery, Carey Todd (1970)
Evans, Richard T., Jr. (1949)
  Evans, Ann (1964)
  Evans, Tabb (1969)
  Evans, Kay (1972)

F
Faile, Garth (1972)
  Faile, Erin (1972)
*Ferrell, Elaine Futrell (1938)
*Flannagan, Mrs. Benjamin (1950)
*Flannagan, Nancy (1961)
*Fleetwood, Wilson, Jr. (1952)
*Flora, Margaret B. (1960)
*Flora, Melvin (1965)
Flora, Fred (1965)
  Flora, Mildred (1965)
  Flora, Freddie (1965)
  Flora, Butch (1965)
Forbes, Edwin T. (1947-1949; 1961)
  Forbes, Polly (1947-1949; 1961)
  Forbes, Tommy (1966)

Forbes, Joan (1966)
Forbes, J. M. (1940-1944; 1945)
  Forbes, Mary (1940-1944; 1945)
Forehand, Celia (1918)
Forehand, C. M., Jr. (1937)
  Forehand, Sylvia (1949)
  Forehand, Mac (1965)
  Forehand, Yvonne (1960)
*Francis, Debbie Joyner (1959)
Futrell, Cloyce (1919)
Futrell, Mrs. Dalton (1957)
Futrell, Earlene (1958) .
Futrell, Barbara (?)
Futrell, O. C. (1938)
Futrell, Raleigh (1941)
  Futrell, Delphia (1941)
Futrell, Robert (1946)
  Futrell, Eva (1945)
Futrell, Thelma (1952)
Futrell, William C. (1943)
  Futrell, Florence (1947)

G
Garrison, James G. (1958)
  Garrison, Joyce (1958)
  Garrison, Jimmy (1965)
  Garrison, Lisa (1967)
Gatewood, Herman (1964)
  Gatewood, Aldene (1964)
Gatling, James (1938)
  Gatling, Alice (1943)
  Gatling, Cheryl Anne (1971)
*Gaudette, Faye Tucker (1956)
Gibbs, George E. (1940)
  Gibbs, Norman (1940)
*Gibson, Mike (1970)
*Glover, Mrs. Jack (1949)
Gordon, Homa (1942)
Gray, Jimmy (1964)
  Gray, Lynn W. (1954)
Green, William Irvin (1949)
  Green, Betty (1949)
  Green, Arlene (1973)
*Green, Annie Lois (1951)
*Greene, Dorothy (1949)
Griffin, Dennis (1968)
  Griffin, Louise (1968)
*Griffith, James (?)
Grizzard, Robert (1950)
  Grizzard, Wiley (1950)
  Grizzard, Ruth (1947)

H
*Hale, Lynn Mixon (1951)
*Hall, Barbara Hill (?)
*Hanson, Lela Harrell (1939)
Harmon, Dewey T. (1968)
  Harmon, Ivor Dean (1968)
*Harden, Gene (1953)
Harrell, Penny (1939)
Harris, Mike (1967)

Harris, Trudy Britt (1956-1965; 1972)
*Harris, W. L. (1952)
 *Harris, Lillie Mae (1952)
Hassell, Jack A. (1957)
 Hassell, Alice (1957)
 Hassell, Linda (1963)
Hazelton, George (1971)
 Hazelton, Nancy (1971)
Hedgpeth, Tony (1940)
 Hedgpeth, Jesse (1944)
*Helms, Charles (1962)
*Henderson, Mrs. J. Q. (1942)
Hill, Albert, Sr. (1931)
 Hill, Mildred (1931)
Hill, Albert, Jr. (?)
 Hill, Shirley (1964 ?)
*Hill, Betty Mann (1957)
Hill, Bob F., Sr. (1946)
 Hill, Josie L. (1947)
 Hill, Catherine (1960)
 Hill, Lloyd (1963)
Hill, Bob. F. Hill, Jr. (1957)
Hill, Bruce (1952)
 Hill, Carol (1964)
Hill, Chester (1952)
 Hill, Janet (1952)
 Hill, Chester, Jr. (1965)
*Hill, Christie Early (?)
Hill, Edward (1946)
 Hill, Sara (1946)
 Hill, Sara Frances (1963)
Hill, Harry W. (1945 ?)
 Hill, Helen (1945)
 Hill, Betsy (1960)
Hill, Hiram C., Jr. (1948-1952; 1953)
 Hill, Ruth (1953)
*Hill, Mrs. Hiram C., Sr. (1949)
Hill, James W., Jr. (1947 ?)
 Hill, Lorene (1947)
*Hodges, Grady, Jr. (1963)
 *Hodges, Mrs. Grady, Jr. (1963)
Hodges, Luther S. (1960)
 Hodges, Doris (1960)
*Hodgin, Madelyn P. (1955)
Holland, Joel C. (1939)
 Holland, Violet (1939)
 Holland, Robert (1962)
 Holland, Joel C., Jr. (1961)
Hollomon, G. R. (?)
 Hollomon, Antoinette W. (1915; 1920-)
*Hollomon, George (?)
*Houghton, Milton (1959)
Howell, Carl (1967)
 Howell, Marie (1967)
 Howell, Mitchell (1972)
Howell, Sam (1965)
 Howell, Betty (1965)
 Howell, Teresa (1965)
 Howell, Sandra Jewel (1971)
Howell, William (1938)
 Howell, Marion (?)
*Hunter, David (1959)
*Hunter, Frank (1940)

*Hunter, Mickey (1951)
Hunter, Richard (1940)
Hunter, Beula (1944)
Hunter, Joe (1963)
*Hutchison, Wilma (1967)

J

Jackson, Roger R. (1965)
Jackson, Alma (1965)
Jackson, Maurice (1966)
Jackson, Eric (1966)
Jackson, Emily (1970)
*Jenkins, Mrs. J. L. (?)
Jenkins, J. M. (1929)
 *Jenkins, J. M., Jr. (1961)
Jenkins, P. Ronald (1950)
 Jenkins, Katherine (1960)
 Jenkins, Nancy (1970)
Johnson, Raleigh (1958)
 Johnson, Sarah (1958 ?)
*Johnson, Shirley Bateman (1955)
*Johnson, Tommy (1959)
Jones, Hattie Russell (1969)
Jones, Thomas L. (1953)
 *Jones, Frances (1958)
 *Jones, Betsy (1959)
 *Jones, Ann (1960)
 *Jones, Tommy (1963)
Joyner, Irvin, Jr. (1939)
 Joyner, Beth (1965)
 Joyner, Berry (1966)
 Joyner, Mike (1972)
Joyner, Jerry (1959)
Joyner, John (?)
 Joyner, Dolly (1964)
Joyner, Mrs. Irvin, Sr. (1961)

K

Kenney, Paul (1961)
*Knight, Cheryl Kay (1964)

L

*Lawrence, Mrs. C. C. (1914-?; 1930)
Lewis, Clayton (1968)
 Lewis, Mary Alice (1968)
 Lewis, Hugh (1968)
Lewter, John L. (1942)
 Lewter, Edna (1942)
 Lewter, Steve (1965)
 Lewter, Gail (1966)
Lewter, Penny (1956)
Liverman, Maggie (1958)
Liverman, George (1955)
Liverman, V. J. (1958)
 Liverman, Juliette (1945)
Long, J. M. (1967)
 Long, Roy Mae (1967)
 Long, Mary (1967)
 Long, Betty (1967)
Lowe, B. Franklin, Jr. (1964)
 Lowe, Peggy (1964)
*Lucus, Lisa Moore (1963)

M

*Mabry, Eva Mae Davis (1960)
McAuley, Terrance (1943)
  McAuley, Hattie (?)
McCraw, William (1963)
  McCraw, Frances (1963)
  McCraw, Debra (1969)
McFadden, Glynn (1956)
  McFadden, Poola (1956)
  McFadden, Keith (1965)
  McFadden, Glynda (1972)
*McLawhorn, Mrs. Allen (1947)
Mann, Betty (1941)
  *Mann, Joan Rae (1962)
Marks, Benny (1957)
Marks, Ed (1962)
Marks, Robert (1953)
  Marks, Ruth (1953)
Martin, E. S. (1949)
  Martin, Mildred (1956)
Matthews, Donna (1968)
*Maxton, Mrs. Harold (1941)
*Meena, Vickie (?)
*Midgett, Marilyn Futrell (1956)
Mixon, Daisy Lou (1951)
Moore, Ivan (1968)
  Moore, Jennifer (1968)
  Moore, Terry (1965)
*Moore, Martha Walker (1961)
Moose, Jessie (1966)
  Moose, David (1966)
*Morrisette, Clayton (1960
  *Morrisette, Betty (1960)
  *Morrisette, Don (1967)
*Moser, Harold (1963)
*Moss, Ruby (1961)

N

*Neal, Sherry (1972)
Nicholson, Nan (1958)
Nicholson, Steve (1958)

O

*O'Brian, Joyce Ann (1946)
Odom, Edward (1920)
  Odom, Doris (?)
*Odom, Mrs. Gene (?)
  *Odom, Kathy (1965)

P

*Palmer, Roxanna S. (1949)
Parker, Alton (?)
  Parker, Jean R. (1960)
  Parker, Al (1973)
Parker, Archie (?)
  Parker, Mamie (1949)
  *Parker, Dianne (1959)
  *Parker, Dickie (1959)
Parker, Bill (1967)
*Parker, Bob (1967)
  *Parker, Mary Beth (1960)
Parker, Carol (1945-1946; 1967)
  Parker, Geri (1945-1946; 1967)

*Parker, David (?)
  Parker, D. L., Jr. (1947 ?)
*Parker, Earl (?)
  Parker, Earl H. (1969)
  Parker, Libba (1969)
  Parker, Jennie Beth (1969)
Parker, Grace (1920)
*Parker, Henry (1967)
Parker, Larry (1959)
Parker, Leonard (1943)
  Parker, Earthleen (1943)
Parker, William D. (1968)
  Parker, Joan (1968)
Paul, Charles L. (1963)
  Paul, Jessie (1963)
Payne, Kate Boyette (1903)
  *Payne, Fred (1939)
*Payne, Hugh (1965)
*Pearce, Ann (1958)
Pennington, J. C. (1967)
  Pennington, Julia (1967)
  *Pennington, Kelly (1967)
Phillips, Bob (1973)
  Phillips, Tommi (1973)
  Phillips, Leisha (1973)
Phillips, Helen (1944)
*Phillips, Mrs. John (?)
Phipps, Edward (1959)
  Phipps, Inez (1959)
  *Phipps, Ronnie (1964)
  Phipps, Faye (1968)
*Phipps, Patrick (1950)
Pierce, Ella J. (1965)
*Pierce, Judy (1961)
*Pipkin, Dennis (1949)
*Pipkin, Ike (1958)
  Pipkin, Ruth (?)
Pipkin, Roswell (1918)
Powers, Jane (1972)
Powers, Jane (1972)
  Powers, Wilson (1972)
*Prather, Carol Beth (1960)
*Pruette, David (1957-1970; 1972)
Pruette, Rowland S. (1956)
  Pruette, Mary V. (1956)

R

*Reavis, Lester (1962)
  *Reavis, Mrs. Lester (1962)
Reed, Mrs. Marion (1955)
*Reed, Teddy (1955)
Revelle, Carson (1958)
  Revelle, Marjorie (1958)
  *Revelle, Dillon (1962)
  Revelle, Allen (1966)
Revelle, Charles L., Sr. (1949)
  Revelle, Martha (1933-1937; 1953 ?)
Revelle, Charles L., Jr. (1949)
  Revelle, Margaret (?)
  Revelle, Chuck (1962)
  Revelle, Meg (1966)
  Revelle, Henry (1973)
Revelle, J. Guy, Jr. (1958)

ReVelle, Gertie (1958)
ReVelle, Gertie (1968)
Revelle, Janie (1961)
Revelle, John P. (1942)
ReVelle, Barbara (?)
ReVelle, Jay (1972)
ReVelle, Dan (1972)
Royce, Phillip (1969)
Royce, Rose Mary (1969)
*Roe, Alice (?)
*Roe, Pearl Bracey (1931)
*Roscoe, Jane Forbes (1959)

S

*Sample, James (1963)
*Samuels, Ed (1972)
 *Samuels, Mrs. Ed (1972)
*Seidmann, Dianne Martin (1956)
Sewell, J. M. (1912)
 Sewell, Thelma (1922)
Sewell, Marjorie (1937)
Sexton, Jean Elizabeth (1971)
Shewbart, Nellie (1945)
*Short, Bettie B. (1939)
*Sidebottom, Patti Shewbart (?)
Simmon,s Carl (1963)
*Smith, Lonnie Sasser (1962)
*Soltes, Ingrid Jo-Ann (?)
Stephenson, James (1949)
 Stephenson, Kathryn (1949)
*Stephenson, James, Jr. (1955)
*Stephenson, Johnny (1956)
*Strange, Norma (1955)
Story, W. T. (1965)
 Story, Mrs. W. T. (1965)
 Story, Billy (1965)
*Styron, Gaye (1963)
Sumner, Eva D. (?)
*Sumner, Patricia Mann (1957)
Sumner, Mrs. Walter (1953)
Sutton, Ben C. (1961)
 Sutton, Minnie (1961)
 Sutton, Ben, Jr. (1968)
 Sutton, Michael (1971)
 Sutton, Steve (1972)
Sykes, I. P. (1942)
 Sykes, Mrs. I. P. (1942)

T

Taylor, R. Hargus (1963)
 Taylor, Doris (1963)
 Taylor, Warren (1971)
*Terrell, Rebekah (1967)
Tillery, Floyd (1946)
 Tillery, Lois (1945)
*Trader, Tommy (1965)
 *Trader, Martha (1965)
*Trader, William (1957)
 *Trader, Mrs. William (1957)
 *Trader, Rickey (1957)
 *Trader, Keith (1965)
Tucker, Harold, Jr. (1947)
 Tucker, Delphia (1957)

Tucker, Mrs. Harold,Sr. (1950)

U

Udvarnoki, Bela (1954)
 Udvarnoki, Ruby Daniel (1954)
*Udvarnoki, Bela, Jr. (1954?)
*Udvarnoki, Gene (1954?)
Underwood, George T. (1954)
 Underwood, Ethleen B. (1928)
*Underwood, Ronald G. (1962)
 *Underwood, Mrs. Ronald G. (1962)

V

Vann, B. Thomas (1969)
 Vann, Mary (1969)
 Vann, Mary (1969)
Vann, Geneva (1954)
Vann, Linwood (1970)
 Vann, Mildred (1970)
Vann, Rabby (1951)
 Vann, Mrs. Rabby (1973)
*Vaughan, Mrs. A. T. (1945)
*Vaughan, Johnny (1940)
*Vaughan, Joseph (1945)
*Vaughan, Robert (1945)
*Vanughan, Mrs. Thomas (1945)
Vincent, Hugh (1959)
 Vincent, Janet (1950)
 Vincent, Dean (1966)
 Vincent, Dane (1966)
 Vincent, Carol (1971)
*Vinson, Gene Parker (?)
Vinson, Melvin (1944)
 Vinson, Edith (1944)
*Vinson, Melvin, Jr. (1949)
Vinson, Patty (?)

W

*Walker, Clifton (1958)
*Warren, David (1961)
Warren, Larry (1962)
Warren, T. K., Jr. ?)
 Warren, Adalee (1951)
 Warren, Tommy (1967)
Watson, B. O. (?)
Webb, Don (1969)
 Webb, Susan (1969)
Whitaker, Bruce E. (1957)
 Whitaker, Esther A. (1957)
 Whitaker, Gary B. (1968)
White, Glenn, Sr. (1950)
 White, Mrs. Glenn, Sr. (1950)
White, Glenn, Jr. (1950)
 White, Joyce (1950)
White, Peggy (1937)
*White, Mrs. Waverly (?)
Whitehead, Mrs. M. E. (1937)
 Whitehead, Eley (1956)
Whitehurst, R. C. (1966)
 Whitehurst, Lucille (1966)
*Whitley, Alice (1939)
*Whitley, Dee (1950)
Whitley, Elmore (1961)

Whitley, Olive (1961)
*Whitley, Elmore, Jr. (1964)
Whitley, Harry (1939)
*Whitley, Harry, Jr. (1964)
Whitley, Randy (1965)
Whitley, James (1949)
Whitley, Mary (1918?)
Whitley, Robert (1921)
Whitley, Mildred (1937)
Whitley, Ruth (1949)
Whitley, Reuben (1949)
Whitley, Sam (1945)
Whitley, Audrey (1926?)
Whitley, Smith (1939)
Whitley, Tee (1939)
Whitley, Sarah (1970)
Whitley, William (1937)
Whitley, Marietta (1950)
*Wiggins, Mrs. C. H. (1946)
Wiggins, C. S. (1946)
Wiggins, Mrs. C. S. (1946)
*Williams, Freda Britt (?)
*Williams, Jimmy (1968)
Williams, W. T. (1947-1950; 1968)
Williams, Dot (1947-1950; 1968)
Williams, Kay (1968)
Williams, Beth (1970)
*Willoughby, Mrs. E. R. (1944?)
*Wilson, Pat (1958)
Wise, Keith (1959)
Wise, Nell (1959)
*Worrell, Bobby (1950)
*Worrell, Eddie (1946)
Worrell, Ray (1946?)
Worrell, Sylvia (1946)
Wooten, Ed (1967)
Wooten, Bobbi (1969)
Wynn, Lois Vann (1910-1915; 1917)

Y

*Young, Tom F. (?)
*Young, Mrs. Tom F. (?)
*Young, Todd (?)

Statistical Data•

Year	Baptisms	Other Additions	Dismissions	Exclusions	Deaths	Total Members
1849	—				—	36
1850	—		—	—	1	27
1851	14	—	—	—	1	40
1852	2	7	3	1		44
1853	14	7	5			60
1854	6		9		—	59
1855	—	—	9	—	—	50
1856	5	2	5		—	52
1857	—	2	2			51
1858	15	5	3		—	64
1859	4	8	5			72
1860	1	3	3			73
1861	8	8	—	—	—	73
1862	15	4	2			85
1863	—		4	—		74
1864			2	3		69
1865			5	4		37
1866	—		1			37
1867	17		5			49
1868		—	4	—		45
1869		—	1	—	—	44
1870	—	5	5	'	2	42
1871	3	—	3		1	40
1872	29	3	8			64
1873	—	3	11			57
1874	13	5	2			81
1875	2	1	3		—	97
1876	32		5		2	107
1877	—		14		—	89

Year	Baptisms	Other Additions	Dismissions	Exclusions	Deaths	Total Members
1878	2	4	3		—	85
1879	—	3	6		5	130
1880		2	18		2	90
1881	1	3	4		—	93
1882	15	14	14		.	97
1883	5	3	12		4	88
1884	14	6	5		2	103
1885	18	5	16	—	1	109
1886	13	8	25	6	—	99
1887	3	—	13	1	2	86
1888		5	10			88
1889		2	8			83
1890		4	6	—		89
1891	—	—	3	2		83
1892	8	13	6	1		98
1893	6	8	2		.	107
1894	15	8	13		1	116
1895	1	4	3	3	2	113
1896	—	7	10	11	3	96
1897	17	13	21	1	4	100
1898	—	11	11			99
1899	5	6	3	—		101
1900	—	2	3	5		94
1901	11	5	4	2	—	104
1902	.	4	5	1	3	100
1903	1	12	5		1	106
1904	10	8	2	—	—	120
1905	10	11	2	4	1	114
1906	5	3	7	—	1	114
1907	8	8	14			115
1908			6			109
1909		4	11			107
1910		8	8			111
1911	4	12	10			94
1912	6	8	5			113
1913	8	21	5			133
1914	—	16	14			131
1915	1	11	9			126
1916	12	10	12			122
1917	—	4	7			115
1918	—	17	14			116
1919	2	12	10			108
1920	10	29	5			136
1921	20	13	9			168
1922	—	12	8			164
1923	.	15	6			175

Year	Baptisms	Other Additions	Dismissions	Exclusions	Deaths	Total Members
1924	—	25	3	—	1	180
1925	2	13	17			174
1926	12	26	14		3	194
1927	6	10	25			185
1928		9	14		1	192
1929	9	5	3		1	175
1930	8	7	6		3	184
1931	7	5	4		—	192
1932	12	8	13		—	188
1933	8	9	5		2	193
1934	—	2	8		—	180
1935	2	11	7		2	184
1936	18	14	5		2	209
1937	3	15	7		3	217
1938	—	7	6	—		217
1939	19	9	2	1		241
1940	22	13	7	—	1	268
1941	1	17	8	—	2	276
1942	7	28	14		3	294
1943	8	26	9	—		318
1944	17	21	11	—	1	344
1945	10	19	7	3	2	361
1946	3	4	8	—	5	356
1947	35	19			3	403
1948	—	7	12		3	395
1949	7	13	17		— a	398
1950	11	16	24		—	391
1951	28	16	24		—	411
1952	4	12	23			406
1953	21	29	17			451
1954	13	25	14			474
1955	27	19	28		—	490
1956	17	24	26			475
1957	9	29	27			490
1958	20	24	18			521
1959	17	31	15			554
1960	16	30	25			575
1961	10	29	26	—		588
1962	13	26	22			605
1963	13	35	—			620
1964	14	25	—			637
1965	22	23	21			661
1966	24	26	41			671
1967	9	24	23			667
1968	10	28	20			683
1969	6	30	30			695

Year	Baptisms	Other Additions	Dismissions	Exclusions	Deaths	Total Members
1970	9	17	19			702
1971	5	8	34			682
1972	9	11	22			680

• All figures are taken from the annual reports to the Association; some errors were probably made in transmission to the annual minutes.

a Separate rosters on deaths not recorded in associational minutes after 1948.

b No figures on dismissions recorded in associational records in 1962—1963

PHOTOGRAPHS OF PASTORS OF
MURFREESBORO BAPTIST CHURCH

George Matthias Thompson
1842-1848

PHOTOGRAPH

NOT

AVAILABLE

Martin Rudolph Forey
1849-1851

Robert Henry Land
1852-1855

Archibald McDowell
1855-1873; 1875-1879

John Mitchell
1873-1875; 1880-1882

Richard Tilman Vann
1883

Charles Wesley Scarborough
1884

Thomas Granberry Wood
1885-1893

Samuel Saunders
1893-1898

George Pinckney Harrill
1898-1902

Albert Thomas Howell
1903-1907; 1910-1912

Arthur Columbus Sherwood
1908-1910

Quinton Clarence Davis
1912-1913

William Harston Woodall
1914

Thomas Calvin Keaton
1915-1918

Julius Wesley Whitley
1919-1925

William Richard Burrell
1925-1932

Jesse Coleman Owen
· 1933-1934

John Henry Bunn
1935-1941

Paul Burton Nickens
1941-1943

Junius Linwood Jones
1943-1948

Warren Francis Taylor
1948-1956

Rowland Shaw Pruette
1956-1968

Thomas Herbert Caulkins
1968-___

CPSIA information can be obtained
at www.ICGtesting.com
Printed in the USA
BVHW041428201118
533625BV00009B/884/P